POWER OR DEPRESSION?

Scholarly Articles by Peter Fritz Walter

POWER OR DEPRESSION?

THE CULTURAL ROOTS OF ABUSE

BY PETER FRITZ WALTER

Published by Sirius-C Media Galaxy LLC

113 Barksdale Professional Center, Newark, Delaware, USA

Set in Avenir Light and Trajan Pro

Designed by Peter Fritz Walter

ISBN 978-1-517321-87-1

Publishing Categories
Psychology / Psychopathology / Depression

Publisher Contact Information
publisher@sirius-c-publishing.com
http://sirius-c-publishing.com

Author Contact Information
pfw@peterfritzwalter.com

About Dr. Peter Fritz Walter
http://peterfritzwalter.com

About the Author

Parallel to an international law career in Germany, Switzerland and the United States, Dr. Peter Fritz Walter (Pierre) focused upon fine art, cookery, astrology, musical performance, social sciences and humanities.

He started writing essays as an adolescent and received a high school award for creative writing and editorial work for the school magazine.

After finalizing his law diplomas, he graduated with an LL.M. in European Integration at Saarland University, Germany, and with a Doctor of Law title from University of Geneva, Switzerland, in 1987.

He then took courses in psychology at the University of Geneva and interviewed a number of psychotherapists in Lausanne and Geneva, Switzerland. His interest was intensified through a hypnotherapy with an Ericksonian American hypnotherapist in Lausanne. This led him to the recovery and healing of his inner child.

In 1986, he met the late French psychotherapist and child psychoanalyst Françoise Dolto (1908-1988) in Paris and interviewed her. A long correspondence followed up to their encounter which was considered by the curators of the Dolto Trust interesting enough to be published in a book alongside all of Dolto's other letter exchanges by Gallimard Publishers in Paris, in 2005.

After a second career as a corporate trainer and personal coach, Pierre retired as a full-time writer, philosopher and consultant.

His nonfiction books emphasize a systemic, holistic, cross-cultural and interdisciplinary perspective, while his fiction works and short stories focus upon education, philosophy, perennial wisdom, and the poetic formulation of an integrative worldview.

Pierre is a German-French bilingual native speaker and writes English as his 4th language after German, Latin and French. He also reads source literature for his research works in Spanish, Italian, Portuguese, and Dutch. In addition, Pierre has notions of Thai, Khmer, Chinese and Japanese.

All of Pierre's books are hand-crafted and self-published, designed by the author. Pierre publishes via his Delaware company, Sirius-C Media Galaxy LLC, and under the imprints of IPUBLICA and SCM (Sirius-C Media).

Pierre's Amazon Author Page

http://www.amazon.com/Peter-Fritz-Walter/e/B00M2QN4SU

Pierre's Blog

https://medium.com/@pierrefwalter

CONTENTS

PREFACE

Is Power Evil?

Krishnamurti said in all his writings that power was evil and destructive. What power did Krishnamurti mean?

This is the question we have to ask. Did he mean natural power, or did he imply the perverse thirst for power that comes from powerlessness?

Is power really evil? Is a thunderstorm evil? Is the power of a tiger evil? What is destructive in relationships: the personal power of a person or the very lack of power?

The answer seems evident: it's the latter. It's not power that is destructive but lacking power, repressed power which is *depression*. Repression and depression do not sound so similar for nothing. Every human being, when conscious of their natural potential of power is constructive and loving. The natural awareness of power is necessary and given to us for self-defense, for marking our personal sphere or simply for having enough courage to advance in life.

Striving for power comes about when natural aggressiveness is repressed; only through this repression, upon which our present civilization is based, natural power perverts into depression—and with that becomes a destructive hunger for power.

When that happens, the natural streaming of life with its energy becomes a cold and stiff controlling of life and also of sexual desire. This obsession for control that goes along with mainstream culture is the result of a lost continuum. When the natural balance is disturbed and power and emotions become repressed, the peaceful continuum that is our natural condition as intelligent human beings is destroyed. The result is fear, the fear of our own destructiveness.

You can compare the perversion of power and its replacement by depression, by sadistic control, with the retrogradation of a planet.

Retrogradation of a planet in astrology means that the energy of the planet, during the phase of retrogradation, is internalized, or interiorized. This energy then cannot be used consciously and its manifestation in life seems to be blocked. There is no success, one feels like an outsider, one is 'not wired' for social acceptance and advancement; with one word: one is not lucky. This image from astrology can be used generally for describing the bioenergy.

For the healthy and positive development of the child it is necessary that the élan vital, or bioenergy, or what I have come to call emotional flow, is streaming; it is essential that this steady flow of the vital energies does not stagnate, as is the case when the energy is caught in the turmoil of fear, worry and guilt.

What happens in this case is that the energy inverts, primarily socially but then also sexually: a sociable child becomes a retired, lonely fellow, a happy child becomes timid, scared, awkward, clumsy, maladroit; a child who was naturally attracted by the other sex begins to exhibit homoerotic attraction. The child that was once gay, becomes 'a gay.'

This is often the result of cruel punishment or religious taboos that provoke guilt and block the psychosexual development of the child temporarily or permanently. The child begins to think before acting, instead of doing things intuitively and elegantly, and thus spontaneity and creativity are going to nuts: the child builds a protective shell and retreats into it for most of the time.

Such a retrogradation of the bioenergetic flow, which results in sexual and non-sexual sadism, is not only the result of sudden attacks such as punishments or abuse, but often generally the result of prudish child-rearing and a strong family focus upon 'Behave yourself!' and a rigid moralistic behavior code.

In cultures where children live their sexuality freely with other children, such as for example the Trobriand culture of Papua New-Guinea, homoerotic inversion is a very rare thing to happen for the child in that culture passes nights from age three in a community dormitory together with other children—and there reigns sexual promiscuity.

Emotional and sexual maturity of the child is thus the result of the child's direct contact with other children as sexual mates. The parents refrain from interfering in any way in the natural emosexual growth process and thus grant their children an utmost amount of autonomy.

In our Western civilization, obviously, things are very different, and this since many generations, to be precise, since about 5000 years, and under the reign of patriarchy, while we have indications that before that time, children were granted more sexual latitude.

Still in the Middle-Ages, as I show in 'Minotaur Unveiled,' matters were simple: a pubescent child was a child that was considered an adult. Sexual maturity was matching social maturity; marriage took place at around twelve years of age and at fourteen a boy reached craftsmanship in his chosen field, thus, puberty concurred with initiation into adulthood—and this seems to me a wise and sustainable social policy.

—See Peter Fritz Walter, Minotaur Unveiled: A Historical Assessment of Adult-Child Sexual Interaction, Scholarly Articles, Vol. 13 (2015/2017).

And how is it today? 'At thirty still in pampers,' I would boil it down to modern jargon, and not without a grain of humor of course. But there is more than a grain of wisdom in that saying. International consumer culture is founded upon the Oedipal Drama which exactly coincides with the *Drama of the Gifted Child*, as Alice Miller put it so brilliantly in her book with the same title.

—Alice Miller, The Drama of the Gifted Child: In Search for the True Self (1996).

This pathology that ranges from parent-child codependence and emotional abuse to schizophrenia and childhood psychosis develops only, as Sigmund Freud found, if culture prohibits free child sexuality. It was also because of Reich's vehement opposition that Freud thoroughly reconsidered the question and eventually told Reich that culture has to prevail.

Which culture, one may want to ask? How can one call 'culture' a system of repression that is clearly perverting the permissive intelligence of nature?

Of course, this book is not an essay about culture. Our task is to penetrate into the in tricate complex of problems that result from this fundamental setup of our culture and to describe the insights that come up regarding depression and its numerous secondary pathologies such as sexual violence, striving for dominance, high divorce rate, lack of emotional and sexual integration, lack of autonomy, unhealthy dependency among family members, rampant abuse, domestic violence, identity problems, narcissism, high suicide rate among children and youth, alcoholism, and others.

INTRODUCTION

The Great Confusion

In our culture, children, because natural partner-sexuality is forbidden to them, have to go through a very strange if not perverse kind of psychosexual development which is marked by a total sacrifice of sexual satisfaction and acceptance of an *ersatz* in form of gerontophilic attraction to their parents.

The child is requested to accept their parents as *ersatz mates* for the sexual relations forbidden to minors—see the association of this enslaving term with minor, minus, minuscule, minority, and mining.

The child is supposed to fall in love to their parent of the opposite sex, and not only platonically, because the libido cannot develop if there is no real sexual stimulus. This clearly incestuous demand of a perverted culture is veiled behind elegant formulas such as Freud's famous 'identifications.' The child has to perform something, not intercourse, but identifications! While normally in life people learn things by doing them, it is said regarding the psychosexual development of the child that in this area things are exactly reversed: the less a child was sexually active, the more healthy was his or her psychosexual growth. As a result, it is supposed that in this case the later adult was able to maintain lasting relations with a monogamous partner of the opposite sex.

Apart from the abstruse logic and mysticism of this construct, statistics clearly speak a another language. With the Trobriands divorce is about 4%, in our society, divorce rates in some regions jump over 80%, in the meantime. With the Trobriands, sexuality is more or less free of partial drives and perversions, and violent sex crimes are non-existent.

In our societies every third asks for psychotherapy because of sexual dysfunctions, frenetic partner change, frigidity or infertility, and sexual crime is rampant. In addition, erectility problems are on rise with males and sadomasochistic inclinations with both sexes. Freud's observation was correct. The civilization child has no choice but to become a gerontophile. And beyond Freud, I add: the sexually mutilated civilization adult has no choice but to become a pedophile!

Next comes the heterosexual altar of cultural purity by cutting out his or her sexual tongue: the child becomes sexually mute, a sexual idiot that later is only able to rape, but not to copulate in a loving embrace.

This perversion of the natural child into a sexually illiterate moron is effected both through an inner process that Freud called identification, and through social hypnosis and the conditioning of the child upon industrially fabricated toys that gradually alienate the child from their own body, their own continuum.

It is argued that it was natural that a boy wanted to be like his father and a girl like her mother, but the truth is of course that no child wants to become a tin-soldier clone of their parents. This truth is veiled because it is not politically correct in a culture of hierarchical subordination in which the younger is supposed to clone the older. It is not politically correct in a culture of industrial manipulation in which the individual is legitimate only in his or her residual habit as a consumer and not through their plain autonomy as a self-thinker and self-feeler.

Freud explained. The first identification is the one that he called homosexual identification: the child identifies with the parent of the same sex. Next comes the heterosexual identification with the parent of the opposite sex, and it's here where Freud spoke of the *Oedipus Complex.*

So, extrapolating this idea, it becomes clear that psychosexually, we are all homosexual because our society denies free child sexuality. More precisely, this latent homosexuality in our culture is the result of social manipulation and not the outcome of natural growth or of choice!

This latent homosexuality becomes real, as a behavior model, when we remain caught in the oedipal trap, when, for whatever reason, we miss the magic jump into the mainstream pool of heterosexuality, or when we not even pass into the oedipal phase.

Here, you should wake up and say: 'Hey! Nature cannot have meant this to happen!' As nature did indeed not mean this to happen, something must be wrong in the way we handle nature, in the way we distort nature.

If you still can think on the lines of natural logic, you should pursue: 'Something is wrong here from the start. It must have to do with the fact that the child is psychosexually conditioned upon their parents instead of being free to engage in sexual play with peers or other adults than the parents as love partners.'

Our culture has institutionalized incest. It makes no difference that lip service is paid to condemning incest as wrong and abject, because what culture says is of little or no impact. What culture does, however, is.

It is equally of no relevance that this incest may not be acted out sexually. I am talking here about emotional incest—and this is the only really destructive incest, as it is impeding the child from growing into autonomy and it is socially sanctioned through patriarchy, the authority principle and forced consumption!

The so-called *Oedipal Phase* in the psychosexual development of the child which usually takes place between the fifth and seventh year, results in the child's *heterosexualizing* their sexuality through attraction to the parent of the opposite sex, while at the same time the homosexual attraction to the parent of the same sex loses importance.

Heterosexuality thus, in this system, comes about only if the child lives successfully through both identifications; only in this case is the child able to gradually get out of the symbiosis with the matrix and to develop true individuality.

It is obvious that our concept of heterosexuality is based upon an almost unbelievable distortion of nature and that this kind of artificial heterosexuality is rather fragile.

Natural heterosexuality is something essentially different. It is heterosexuality that I qualify as *manifest*, brought about by natural intercourse and love between partners of the opposite sex, and this as early as possible in the life of the person.

Our society's concept of heterosexuality is schizoid. It considers as normal the premature homosexual and gerontophilic conditioning of the child that is forced upon the child.

I have explained this once to a little boy. He has understood immediately what I was talking about and replied:

—I won't collaborate in their sordid system. Let them come. I do not let myself distort by them. They anyway love dogs more than children, and when they love children, it's only because they need us as lightning catchers because they never get along among each other, and pass their lives in endless domestic fighting!

If we consider life, as it is taught by quantum physics, as a sequence of synchronistic processes and probabilities, it becomes evident that it is more probable to remain caught in one's *Oedipus Complex* than to liquidate it. It is for example as good as impossible for the child to liquidate their Oedipus if the parent of the opposite sex is either dead, absent or unacceptable.

And how many single-parent families there are today, and the number grows exponentially with every year!

One result of this social reality is that there is a mutation in the psychosexual development of children, more and more also on a global level. A lacking father is a lacking father, however the mother tries to replace the father, as many mothers think they had to, ignorant about the fact that they pervert the child even more through such behavior, especially when the child is a boy. Neurotic mothers are phallic witches for their male children in an eternal drama of the gifted child who will at the end of the day kill their mothers—as Nero did! But most do it not physically, but symbolically, namely by suiciding themselves, or by raping, torturing or strangling a little girl, by substance abuse and alcoholism, by throwing down an elder from a bridge:

—Sorry, man, this had to happen after all!

In this constellation the sexual energy inverts: it is directed inside instead of outside, inward instead of outward, within the body instead of outside of the body.

The rape victim has put her life inside her body and the rape symbolically liberates her life from that body that enclosed it. That is the logic of rape, seen from the side of the passive partner. From the side of the active partner, rape is the desire to liberate oneself from oedipal constriction through liberating another from exactly the same constriction.

Rape is a linguistic misunderstanding. The word 'rape' literally means theft. It is a symbolic act of taking back what one believes to have lost, that is, one's sexual innocence. In depriving a child of sexual innocence, the rapist symbolically puts himself in a renewed state of purity, of innocence. Through the rape of another, he is 'less raped' himself.

But what mainstream psychology never has understood is that the rapist also liberates the victim from a denial of living, and through forced copulation tells the victim that life is copulation! This is how the rapist renews and strengthens the victim's survival responses. Interestingly, many more rapists commit suicide after raping than rape victims after being raped!

The child, in many cases, cannot do that magic jump into heterosexuality that comes about through mastering the oedipal constriction. Hence, the child remains in the previous condition of psychosexual development, that of anal-sadistic homosexuality. When the child gets stuck in the oedipal trap or, to put it differently, gets caught in the spider web of the homosexual labyrinth, the fusion with the matrix becomes definite, and in most cases is no more reversible.

This fusion that I call 'secondary fusion' is then transported into adolescence where it is fed by higher sexual energy and will manifest through one or the other form of sexual violence.

This explains why violent emotions such as hatred, anger or revenge feelings get linked to sexual arousal. A once overtly timid boy becomes a notorious rapist who considers his penis as a weapon and sexuality as an erotic shooting exercise.

These emotions are so present because the eternal marriage with mother that is forced upon the boy-child in our culture—and other cultures that are even worse than ours, such as India—creates an irresistible rage that will become linked to sexual arousal. In extreme cases, sexual arousal, then, cannot be experienced anymore without a secondary emotion such as rage, or without humiliating the sexual mate through physical threat and/or beatings or other forms of torture. It is clear that until lust-murdering a mate, there is only a tiny step to take, and for this step our perverse education prepares very well!

That most of us do not rape and murder shows that we steer rather effectively against this general trend in our culture, that we as individuals are actually more virtuous and more human than our culture is.

And that we have built an almost heroic self-discipline, where creatures of lesser stature than humans would perhaps leap into error and annihilate a whole culture.

Of course, the right and effective solution here would be to change the entire concept of mainstream education, both in the West and the East.

The child needs to be free to realize their sexual nature and to express it through physical copulation, actively and passively. This is part of the eternal yin-yang of the whole cosmos. Thus, this is not only a psychological idea, but part of a political agenda!

Without this fundamental step away from moralism and toward love, we will not be able to realize world peace in any scenario of a future society.

This terrible rage as a result of lacking autonomy is to be explained as an infantile reaction, as a primal sensation that has survived childhood and became rooted in adulthood: in reality it is the fear of death! For in every life-in-growth there is a strong will for autonomy: it is the will to pass the growth process as soon as possible and to become as those who are grown-up.

Once a child feels that mother wants child back in the womb, wants child remain a dwarf, a puppet and partial object of mother's larger body, child will feel threatened in their life. Life for a child is a synonym for growth and if growth is not allowed, life is not allowed. Such a child rightly gains the conviction that his or her mother wishes child to be dead or return into the womb—which boils down to be the same.

Why does a mother act like that, one may want to ask? Because she herself remained infantile, and instead of being a mirror for her child, only mirrors herself narcissistically.

The problem becomes very complex through the fact that the child cannot consciously integrate or express the terrible anger at the witch-mother. This feeling must remain tabooed for the child as it

triggers a survival response: the child is horrified at
the thought of questioning the source of their safety
and daily care. This is why this rage is repressed into
the deepest layers of the unconscious where it leads a
shadow existence like the mythical Minotaur.

One day, the charmed frog will be liberated
through the love of a princess. The liberation comes
about through the energy of love. Love retransforms
Minotaurean energies back into constructive vital
energies. Love is an alchemistic process of the highest
effectiveness; it means unconditional acceptance of
one's own desire and at the same time the
acceptance of the desire of each and every other
individual.

To split love off into categories of filial love,
platonic love, erotic love, friendship, enemy love, god
love and other nonsense destroys love. Love cannot
be divided. All sexual taboos are equally love taboos.
When citizens in a country spy each other out, trust is
not possible and this is the reason that today in
postmodern international culture, which is a
fundamentally moralistic culture, children grow again
in a climate of anguish, strife and persecution that is
directly opposed to their healthy emosexual growth.

This insight should help us reconsider the taboo of child sexuality, and the further taboo of erotic love between children and adults. The reason for this reconsideration is that intergenerational love outside of the family is an effective way out of the oedipal dilemma.

This form of love plays an initiatory role in social relations and represents a constructive possibility of fostering the growth of autonomy and personal power. To bring this about, an end of sexual hypocrisy is needed; in addition we have to research the benefits of intergenerational love and sex-economic child-rearing, as well as the end of sexist ideas and the repression of emotions.

Especially important in education is the integration of the *anima* with boys and the *animus* with girls, the assimilation of the other half, in order to get at a harmonious relationship of yin and yang. Present education, however, represents systemic debilitation of emosexual wholeness and creates a high anxiety potential in the young generations of tomorrow. However, with fear no problem can be solved, and no loving world can be created, and no natural and conscious relationship with the environment can be built. Worse, fear cuts the connection with our higher self, the true and authentic identity of the individual.

Fear creates an authority-craving, opportunist and weak character that is prone to manipulation and collective lies in what ideological costume ever they appear. If the world is to survive, we must bring about the exact opposite characteristics in the young generations. This is not possible without raising our emotional awareness, as I have pointed this out in all my writings on human evolution and sociopolitical policy making.

—See, for example, Peter Fritz Walter, The 12 Angular Points of Social Justice and Peace: Social Policy for the 21st Century, 2015/2017.

The present study erects the hypothesis that love and depression are mutually exclusive. Where love is, depression must fade. Where depression is, love cannot be. Love is power, natural and non-destructive power. But this power of love has nothing in common with social or economic power. It is a love-specific power. I call it primary power.

We speak about the power of love. This power is equal to the power of life which is love. Life is love.

The power of love can be compared with the power of art or the power of wisdom. For here we also speak about powers that are beneficial and not the destructive power that is the result of depression.

This is so because the powers of love, of art or of wisdom are not dominating or exploiting their objects; they are innocent in the true sense of the word, in-nocent, not harming, and because they are free of guilt. It is a fatal error by puritanical minds to see power abuse as immediately inherent in sexuality.

Through this error, that has been partly corrected by sexology, a sex-hostile morality and culture was built, especially in Western society, that has created havoc.

The present study will show what I understand under primary power, integrated power, or self-power, as I call it, and why it is essential for building and maintaining constructive and harmonious relationships among people. And I will demonstrate what exactly is depression, and show that depression was systematically bred since the beginning of patriarchy, and what mess it has created in our society, and what the consequences are that we are facing today and tomorrow, and that our children are going to face for many generations to come.

CHAPTER ONE

Breeding Depression

INTRODUCTION

Socrates said the only thing he knew something about was love. Was it for this reason that he never was interested in a power position in the Greek government and instead preferred walking through the streets and asking people intriguing questions? Was Socrates claiming an other-worldly power?

It is noteworthy that also Jesus of Nazareth came along with the idea that his power was not from this world. When we consider his modest birth and youth, this man certainly did not irradiate worldly power.

If we further look at the life of the Buddha, we see a man who at first was very powerful socially but then resigned this power and became a *sannyasi*, a wandering hermit.

Can we conclude that Socrates, Jesus and Buddha were powerless? And how was it with Gandhi? These men certainly had power, greater power than all worldly forces at their lifetimes. But what was the kind of power they had?

Let us look, on the other hand, at the gruesome life of a man called Adolf Hitler. What kind of power did he have? Did he have power? Or was the horror that he brought about not the result of blind rage, of an immensely pent-up depression? In German depression is called *Ohnmacht* which means 'Without Power' and thus can be translated as non-power.

Is not every abuse of power a use of non-power, of depression? What is it that triggers destructiveness? Is it power or is it depression or non-power?

When we look at powerful wild animals such as tigers or lions, or even very large animals such as elephants, we see how incredibly tender they are when tendering (sic!) their young, how much care they bestow upon their offspring, how lovely they foresee to avoid the smallest shortcomings that could bring displeasure to their young!

What is it that animates these animals, power or depression? Without any doubt, the motor of this great natural intelligence is power.

And how is it with the power of our worldly rulers and dignitaries? Do they really have power? Or do they reign with non-power, with depression?

Was Napoleon powerful? Or was he a depressive dwarf whose megalomania was reversely proportional to his inferiority complex?

In hexagram thirty-four of the I Ching, Da Dchuang —Power of the Great (34), we read: 'The common man reigns through power, the noble not.' The interpretation explains: 'The power is not to be seen outside but it can move heavy load such as a truck which is strong because of its axis. The lesser power is used on the outside level, the greater it is.'

Should our focus thus be to scrutinize if power is used on the inside or the outside level, if it is used for self-development or for the molding of the outside world?

Let us consider the power of a hermit. Such a man has evidently no worldly power. He even shuns any manifestation of external power. But does he not have a strong inner power, an immense inner power even, an inner power so great that it can spiritually transform the whole world in less than a lifetime? And when we listen to the pianist Svjatoslav Richter, do we not wonder about the great power of his art?

To end this circle of questions, let's consider a moment the insights we gain from psychiatry and psychoanalysis. What is the goal of every therapy? Is it not to help the patient build primary power, self-power or soul power, to help him or her deal with dependency patterns and to positively sustain his or her quest for autonomy?

Of course, these are rhetoric questions and the answers come up intuitively as you ponder the questions, and without further effort.

With this in mind I would like to have a deeper look at outside power, and especially how power is acted out in relationships. Our regard will first be a general one, then we will focus upon sexuality as an important part of human relations.

Let me start with a work hypothesis. Later in this study I will try to produce evidence that may corroborate, or not, my hypothesis. I suggest that destructive power in relationships is always, there is always composed of three elements that are present in one or in both partners of the relationship:

▸ Lack of autonomy;

▸ Confusion about the boundaries of the body;

▸ Deep and lasting depression.

Besides that, I will show in this study that traditional education, as it was monopolized by church and state, has systemically bred all three factors and therefore is largely responsible for the mess we face today in the world.

As examples to the contrary I will refer to the tribal cultures of the North American Indians, the natives of South America and some Nomadic cultures such as the Tuareg who respect the person or light body of the child in a way industrial culture never did.

These tribal cultures also favor autonomy and personal identity in their child-rearing practice, while postmodern international consumer culture encloses the child in a protective shell that suffocates the child's emotional and sexual life. To put it in still simpler terms, I say that tribal cultures favor and care for a basic continuum that can be translated into the slogan 'Life is Love.' On the other hand, modern industrial world culture is to be characterized, very similar to the Roman empire, by the slogan 'Life is Power.'

Both paradigms bring about social realities and political strategies and policies that are quite different, not to say incompatible with each other.

THE MAGIC SPELLS

Before producing evidence for the hypothesis that I pointed out in the previous paragraph, let us see what in detail breeds depression and how it is brought about in the youth.

Transactional Analysis (TA) revealed to what extent traditional education uses suggestions in order to mold the child according to social norms and expectations.

Suggestions are hypnotic formulas that are written in the child's mind through what is called magic spells.

Some of these spells are:

▸   Be ideal!

▸   Remain small and helpless!

▸   Remain unclear about who you are!

An adult who appears in front of the child as a god-like and infallible creature, or as an 'ideal parent,' suggests even without words, that the child, compared with such example of human perfection, is unendingly sinful, stupid, weak, and powerless. Each of us who has been reared by such an example of embodied virtue and infallibility, be it in their vintages as parent or educator, knows what I am talking about.

Carl Gustav Jung said that the cabinets of psychoanalysts are filled with people who had 'ideal parents.'

Education based upon ideals always tends to idealize not only certain ideologies or a certain Weltanschauung, but also people. An idealized human is not a real human. And this is valid so much the more for children because children think in real and not in ideal categories.

Ideals are abstract ejaculations of thought that the child's mind cannot bring about nor embrace. And fortunately so! Ideals may have a certain moral value, but in education they are not only worthless, but really destructive. And this because they pervert the child's psyche through their pretension to represent truth.

What is truth? Only the mature mind of an adult, allow me to say this *cum grano salis*, disposes of enough objectiveness to recognize the relativity of every ideal and thus to grasp that ideals always are part-truths but never 'the truth.'

Depression always refers to a single ideal, be it fundamental-religious or political-ideological, that violates the unconditioned wisdom of the child. Repressive and obsessively coercive education can realize its sordid goals only through sublime psychic terror, and this terror primarily focuses upon the child! This was known by tyrants of all times until today.

Etymologically I am speaking here about ideologies and not about ideals, and while I am well aware of the theoretical difference, at the end of the day, believe me, all boils down to the same; for every ideal can be converted or perverted into a life-denying ideology or into religious tyranny.

Not only in Antiquity but as well in our days millions of people are sacrificed for ideals. All wars, in the whole of human history, have been fought for ideals. Hitler's Nazi ideology is based upon an ideal of racial purity, the horrors of communist persecution and torture were founded upon well-sounding ideals of social reform, the destruction that the Cultural Revolution in China has caused to the cultural heritage of humanity was motivated by ideals. The cruelty of the Crusades and the Inquisition or the French Revolution were founded upon religious and political ideals—and so forth without end. Cruelty, persecution, wars, civil wars and the countless massacres of minorities can only end when we understand that the so-called 'evil' in the world cannot be ended through ideals, nor through moral wars or anti-drug campaigns, but only through a revolution of consciousness that is not based upon the mental creation of ideals. Great sages such as Maharshi or Krishnamurti have shown us the way.

J. Krishnamurti has given us a detailed account of a non-repressive and creative education to wholeness, an education that has an immediate link with truth, with life, and that avoids as much as possible the intellectual trap that is so typical for idealistic education.

—See J. Krishnamurti, Education and the Significance of Life (1978).

Let me now discuss in detail some of the magic spells that are part of life-denying education, and show their destructive impact upon the child's psyche.

BE IDEAL!

To ask something impossible from somebody inevitably brings about in that person a sensation of powerlessness, an acute feeling of non-power, of depression. This is so much the more true when the asker possesses higher social power than the person who is asked. And when we look at the relationship society-child, this is still of much higher impact.

When Adolf Hitler was a small boy, his father treated him like a cockroach. The result was that little Adolf became an insect that devoured almost the whole of Europe. The research conducted by the Swiss psychoanalyst Alice Miller has delivered valuable insights into Hitler's childhood as well as the childhood of Jürgen Bartsch, the German serial child killer that made history in the 1960s.

—See Alice Miller, Hidden Cruelty in Child-Rearing and the Roots of Violence (1983), Thou Shalt Not Be Aware (1998) and The Political Consequences of Child Abuse (1998).

Jürgen Bartsch, abandoned by his parents in early childhood, grew up with a foster family who ran a butchery. It was a gruesome couple. The adoptive mother used to throw butcher knives after little Jürgen when he failed in one of his tasks—because he had to work from babyhood.

Human nature is not bad from birth and therefore does not need to be 'improved' by religions or political ideologies; what such oppressive systems of manipulation result in is simply to further deteriorate the human condition still further. Were such systems really motivated by deep trust in a beneficial creator force, what name you wish to give to it, they never had upheld the abstruse idea that this potential benefactor-power creates a human that, as they assume, was bad from birth—blemished with 'original sin.' If man, as I assume, and the whole of creation is naturally good and blessed, all our emotions are good and important and must be integrated in the whole of life.

This requires us to accept their existence, and that we foster their creative expression! Not more and not less, for all that we wish to express is already born into us, from our beginnings, and regardless of our age or gender.

The magic spell *Be Ideal!* that is used for hypnotizing children in the repressive milieu is highly perverting. It suggests to children to not be something that they are and to become something that they should not become, that is, perverse.

Research on the causes of child psychosis and schizophrenia has shown that these most frequent emotional disturbances are bred in a family milieu of extreme dishonesty and hypocrisy where the people around the child typically are sworn into condemning the child as the culprit for the family karma. The verbal and nonverbal messages transmitted to the child usually say exactly the contrary of what the child observes or intuits.

There is no more effective means to condition children than subjecting them to ideals. From there, it's only a step until subjecting them to the tyranny of 'political correctness.' There are so many historical and present examples for this fact that I spare them out here.

REMAIN SMALL AND HELPLESS!

This is a very effective magic spell that virtually inhibits children from growing bigger. Here belong all those messages that ask the child to remain puppet-like, small and cute, thus suggesting to the child that it's better to stay small than to grow.

Dwarfs are often not the result of genetic errors; they often are children under the hypnotic command of remaining small and helpless. They namely obeyed parental instructions word by word.

Their subconscious executed the perverse parental suggestion to keep small and helpless, means: easy to manipulate.

This magic spell that often is used by a lonely mother is very destructive in that it holds the child entrapped in the fusion with the matrix, downplaying every attempt of the child to cut the umbilical bond of dependence.

The child is conditioned into believing that all good relationships are those that foster symbiotic dependence. That is why this magic spell is especially counter-productive to the child's quest for autonomy.

Let me add the remark that a mother who appears to be particularly loving and touchy often is encouraged by her social environment and receives help from all sides, which contributes to strengthen the codependence and abusive relationship she maintains with the child.

This is why, in this kind of constellation, the child regularly receives the hypnotic spells not only from their mother but also from grandparents and other persons who are in favor of the idea that a mother 'should receive compensation' from her child for the refusal of affection and tenderness from the side of her partner. This support in turn encourages her to really use the child as a tear-pillow and poison-container.

—See, for example, Lloyd DeMause, The History of Childhood (1974).

It is true that this phenomenon has been studied quite in detail, also from a sexological point of view. It was shown that for the psychosexual development of the child, such a parental attitude is highly destructive in that it results in sexual impotence with males, and frigidity with females.

The vital energy naturally manifests through a libido that is directed away from the family. And here I obviously contradict Freud. Such a libido cannot develop in a child who intuitively knows that a parent is emotionally dependent upon the strong and exclusive relationship with the child.

This means that parental affection, with emotionally abusive parents, is itself on an infantile level and thus the child is rather playing the role of a parent of their own parent, than being a child of that parent. Such a child will always try to fulfill the emotional demands of the parent-abuser and bury their own need for autonomy. The price for obedience is very high: it's the price of a human life! For the élan vital will retrograde and many of the child's best talents will develop with lots of delay or never. This is what I call emotional abuse!

This complex of pathological symptoms is what I call emotional abuse, and which encompasses physical and sexual abuse, while emotional abuse is the overarching notion.

My view on the matter has in the meantime been taken up and is now shared by a number of qualified child psychologists and abuse experts.

—See, for example, Joel Covitz, Emotional Child Abuse (1986).

I would like to speak in this context of *affective impotence* than of sexual impotence, and this because with most men who have problems with codependence can well have strong erections, if there is no physical handicap.

The problem typically manifests through frequent and even frenetic partner change, fear of closeness, of intimacy, or explosive emotions such as rage, anger or desires for revenge that become linked to sexual arousal, with the result of sadomasochistic urges and resulting perverse behavior.

I already said above that libido inverts if there is no affective link to the parent of the opposite sex, or a parent-replacement, which can be a babysitter or even a child-loving stranger. In this case, the libido inverts and the child will retreat from group life and develop timidity and shame regarding their body; and guilt will dominate the mainly masturbatory sex life. On a cognitive level the child will develop peculiar strange habits such as collecting stamps or insects, or matches, cups, hats, stickers or dead mice, or other tiny objects.

For the child such a development clearly is defeating because it's an *ersatz* for real pleasure; the anal collector obsession demonstrates the regression of genitality into anality. Hence, the child remains on a partial and fragmented developmental stage, without completing their psychosexual growth. Prevailing emotions are anger, frustration and depression.

Typically, in this constellation attempts of the child to gain autonomy, especially regarding erotic relations with peers, or for satisfying sexual curiosity, will be rejected by the pathological possessiveness of the codependent parent; and even if permission is given once in a while, it is usually given in a way that induces even more guilt and shame in the child.

These feelings of depression that are accumulated during the oedipal phase are later transported into adolescence where they risk to be charged with higher sexual energy, and can then potentially in sexual violence.

Boys or girls that are conditioned in this unlucky manner will tend to avoid sexual contacts with the other sex, and often, a conservative or religiously colored vocabulary is used to overtly deny the desire for sexual experiences or the need for sexual abreaction.

Contacts are sought out with the same sex. The latent homosexuality may once in a while surge up into consciousness and a same-sex erotic experience may happen. But in most cases, and depending on the strength of awareness of the person, the homosexual tendency is denied and remains unaware; it will be hidden behind moralistic or even persecutory behavior and over-adaptation which, in turn, alienates the person still farther from her body reality.

If sexuality is accepted or not, the question of power or depression will be important in this situation because it conditions behavior: the young person may either display a snobbish, arrogant and dominant style or in the contrary exhibit a rather slavish, smeary obedience, and in both alternatives there will be a relatively high level of aggressiveness and competitiveness.

I admit that I am generalizing these insights, and know that this needs further scientific corroboration, but say that competitive-aggressive cultures, such as the United States of America are those that, through their puritanical and extremely moralistic life paradigm, more or less systematically breed the compensatory codependence between parents and children.

Remain Unclear Who You Are!

This is another magic spell that serves to disempower the child and alienate them from their body for the abuser-parent to gain more latitude in controlling the child. This magic formula that is induced rather non verbally leads to a deep confusion in the child about the contours of the body, the limits of the ego and generally, the limits in every respect. And there will be daily fuss about limits, and discussions like: 'Stay in your room and don't fool around in my desk. It's not your business! You have your toys, you have your pets, you have your room, period!'

Of course, such clear statements mark a flagrant contradiction to the parents' own behavior, when fooling around in the stuff belonging to the child and without even the slightest attempt to see that the child equally has a privacy sphere that adults need to respect.

To disregard one's limits means that:

  ▸ one tends to manipulate others even without realizing it;

  ▸ one disregards inner signals that show limitations;

  ▸ one tends to treat the body of another as if it was one's own body.

A codependent mother tends to use and abuse parts of the child's body like her own body, taking it for granted that her psyche is eternally fusioned with the psyche of the child. The consequences of such parental attitudes are fatal for the child.

The same is true in some way for the father-child relationship, while the results are less fatal, simply because man is not the matrix that will receive, but spermgiver, and this psychological fact that may seem of minor significance culturally, is highly significant on the level of the child's psyche.

Man is more easily inclined to grant autonomy than woman because woman who cannot conceive anymore will try to receive, attention, veneration, adoration, affection, tender care, emotional comfort and total comprehension. As typically in this constellation, woman does not receive all this from her partner-man, because when man refuses to give sperm, man also refuses to give love and affection, and as a result woman tries to receive it from child as a compensatory agent.

Such a mother will display an excessive demand of consideration and understanding from the side of child or children; she will tend to burden the child with responsibilities and often also induce guilt in the child regarding her being so 'unlucky' in the couple relation.

From here, to ask for complicity in a non-marital because incestuous relationship with the child is only a step; and to repeat it, it's of minor importance that such incest is acted out sexually; it is the psychic component alone that has the devastating impact upon the present and future behavior models of the child.

A child in such a situation namely cannot easily find out who he or she is, thus being impeded from defining and developing their identity, as identity building is only possible when mother's and child's body images have been disentangled and experienced as separated.

Codependent mothers typically do the contrary: in order to keep the original symbiosis with her baby, the fusional mother induces guilt in the child every time the child attempts to gain autonomy, which in turn leads to the child switching forth and back between the desire to gain a distance from mother and again being attracted to her.

This can be easily imagined using the following parable. Represent in your mind mother and child being held by a thin elastic rope: every time child moves centripetally, away from mother, and toward life, the rope is stretched, and stretched more.

The faster and the more impetuously the child runs toward the world, in the firm intent to leave mother, the more brutally the rope will catapult the child back to her, and this means on the psychic level: back into the tranquil matrix and away from a pulsating world.

The elastic rope symbolizes the codependent bond and also shows elegantly that such bond is bondage.

Only he who knows who he is can develop enough personal power to direct their life. Today most young people in postmodern international consumer culture are caught in clinging fusional bondage with their mothers, thus remaining clumsy pampered toddlers for their whole life. It's inevitable to happen in a culture that denies the child their own sexuality. The result is not tears, but big business. The sordid enslavement of the consumer child produces hard dollars worldwide. The sweet comfort and well-to-do safety is the most unheard-of collective form of child rape that ever occurred in history.

Through mother-child codependence in the modern urban culture, and with a father often pushed at the periphery, the holy mother that is the real profiteer in this unjust relation is compensated for her loneliness in the couple relation—because man is busy with business, disqualified collectively as a child-sitter and caretaker.

The one who pays the bill for this absurd and perverse theater is of course the child; the results are schizophrenic tendencies and lasting depression, together with a weak sense of identity are among the results cashed in long-term.

What young people learn instead is to identify with groups, and only very few develop their own firmly established identity through self-knowledge and a self-thinking approach to life and society. The answer I usually get when I say this is:

—But you know, this was always so! True freedom has never existed in human history; children were always enslaved and treated as poison-containers.

It is easy to relativize each and every new insight with the slogan 'this was always so.' This attitude only betrays ignorance regarding the many grey shades of life, and besides that, it's simply not true. Fact is that technology-based civilization progressively prolongs the parent-child dependency, as a matter of socioeconomic reality. At the same time, forms of collective fusion, the growing dependency of emotionally starved youngsters with groups and group life, is ruthlessly exploited by sects and malevolent political groupings because they thank their rank-and-file to society's silent complicity in enslaving the child.

Psychologists tend to justify this state of affairs, arguing that it was our prolonged educational cycle that was at the root of the problem; in addition they note that modern society lacks initiation rites such as tribal cultures do, and that another fatal factor was the taboo on strong father-child relationships and the lack of males in child care, at home and in pre-school education.

This is true, but this situation is not in any way a forcible characteristic of postmodern society, but the direct result of fascist values prevailing in today's international culture. It is typical for all fascist societies to discard men out from the home, binding him to his job, that has to be hard work and not soft childcare, and this tendency is not a historical or social hazard, but the result of fear—the fear that man, and rightly so, may bring in the erotic element into the man-child relation that fascist society so carefully tries to wipe under the carpet.

The number one issue discussed on the hot agenda of all societies that have subscribed to international consumer culture is so-called 'child abuse,' sexual relations between adult males and children, most of them occurring within, and not outside of the family.

Self-determination and acuteness, sharp consciousness, passion, and creativity are all dependent upon a vidid sex life, and when sex is completely repressed, these values pretty much turn into their contrary, and the person begins to crave for authority and domination, like the woman who asks her husband to be raped, because she can't get an orgasm otherwise.

Suffices to see children in religious institutions for orphans, as I saw so many in my life, and around the world, and who constantly smear honey around the mouth who care for them. All in their behavior points to their high amount of fear, and their ingrained conviction to be subordinated under a powerful regulatory and punitive force, a force that once in a while acts out in holocausts when there is time for whipping, for example.

Alternative child psychologists have since long provided striking evidence as to physical torture in an otherwise caring adult-child relationship, provoking strong sexual responses on both educator and student.

Lacking orientation, so often complained about regarding our youth is no wonder in a culture that has itself no real roots because it has become alienated and dysfunctional, lacking out in its foremost duty: to sustain humans in their unique life paths, mission and creativeness. As a result, depression is not only an individual phenomenon but has become something like a collective curse, a group depression. People wish to dominate and emotionally manipulate another because they do not know who they are and are confused about limits.

Rampant traffic delinquency in all our major civilizations today is another indication that my hypothesis bears some truth, because in traffic all is about limits and respecting limits, and traffic is for the unconscious a direct corollary of sexual traffic in the sense of intercourse. Thus, automobile crime, sexual crime and drug traffic have become a whole large area of compensatory action, and corresponding conflict.

And when we look at the behavior of nations, there is further evidence that corroborates my theory. For example, one nation desires to subordinate another because it is depressed. The depression was provoked by a fight about limits, the borders of the nation and those of the other nation.

Border fights are what most often in history provoked wars between nations. International law has developed a vocabulary for these problems that is strikingly similar to psychological language.

For example, international law experts talk about a lack of identity of a certain nation or about lacking self-determination, or about feelings of megalomania that make for a confusion about the borders of the country.

Right-wing law experts in the 1930s in Germany and even abroad claimed public understanding for Hitler's megalomaniac demands to gain back the old Reich that pretendedly was 'stolen' from Germany during World War I. It was argued that in some way Hitler had been right and therefore largely supported in his *Kriegspropaganda* because de facto Germany had been 'punished too harshly' after World War I and therefore 'had been humiliated in its national identity.'

This was the official rhetoric that even today is upheld by some historians, and even those who are not openly justifying fascist ideologies.

In the dealings of nations with each other we encounter exactly the same fights about limits that we know so well from the family therapy practice.

A psychosis is the total crash of all inner boundaries, especially those between inside and outside reality. There is striking evidence that shows the correlation between infantile psychosis and a general lack of boundaries in the family group life the psychotic child belongs to. Boundaries, do what you will, are needed as a base condition for respect. Abusive parents that are not able to give enough empathy and autonomy to their children are abusive in the first place because they confound their body boundaries with those of their children.

As already pointed out previously, incest is exactly based upon this 'possession thinking' so deeply rooted in materialistic society, and patriarchy has established it, no doubt, thousands of years ago, in the relationship between the father, as the *patria potestas*, and all females and female children that inhabit the household. That power to rape-and-enjoy all that is subordinated, except it's male, was also notoriously practiced with slaves, and maids and their girl children. It is a custom that until today can be found in remote regions in various countries in parts of the world, and generally in highly patriarchal societies.

—See, for example, Riane Eisler, The Chalice and the Blade: Our History, Our Future (1995).

From this perspective, incest could be redefined as sexual dominance over all females, regardless of age, contained in the larger household. Incest is originally a non-sexual or rather a pre-sexual matter: it's about power that we are talking.

As the late French psychoanalyst Françoise Dolto put it in one of her books, incest begins where parents rule over the bodies of their children as princes reign over their vassals. Such parents suggest to their children that they do not own their bodies, but that the child's body is owned by the parents of the child.

—See Françoise Dolto, La Cause des Enfants (1985).

Love, and especially when the loving bond is also finding its physical counterpart, is without a doubt the most immediate possibility for any human, and regardless of age, to gain self-knowledge, autonomy and self-determination.

To deny the child physical love is a form of torture and it should be prohibited by law by subsuming such parental attitudes under the United Nations Convention Against Torture.

—The United Nations Convention Against Torture and Other Cruel, Inhuman or Degrading Treatment or Punishment is an international human rights instrument, under the purview of the United Nations, that aims to prevent torture around the world. The Convention requires states to take effective measures to prevent torture within their borders, and forbids states to return people to their home country if there is reason to believe they will be tortured. The text of the Convention was adopted by the United Nations General Assembly on 10th of December 1984 and, following ratification by the 20th state party, it came

into force on 26th of June 1987.
http://www.hrweb.org/legal/cat.html

That today's international culture perversely practices the exact contrary does not invalidate my statement but shows to what point that culture is structurally abusive.

The magic about love is that in each love relation we not only learn to love the object of our love but at the same time a part of ourselves, a part of our own individuality. That mirror effect that magically is contained in the loving bond is tremendously important for our growth process, regardless of age or gender.

Love is a heavenly force for big and small humans alike, for it lets us understand without words that we are all interconnected by an invisible particle intelligence that at the same time connects us to the whole of life in the universe and assigns to each being its own appropriate point in the moving space-time continuum.

Where there is love, desire is holy; where there is love, abuse is not entirely excluded but highly unlikely to happen.

CHAPTER TWO

The Healing Power of Self-Power

In therapy all is setup to catalyze the upsurge of the patient's self-healing power. Let me call this fantastic self-repair potential of the human body here simply self-power or primary power, for notably this power comes from inside, from our center, and it's a genuine power and in no way a product of culture or of education.

Primary power is not granted or transmitted to us but manifestly is a part of our wandering soul, that spirit that incarnates and reincarnates, constantly changing vehicles while remaining unchanged in its spiritual energy code and identity.

And, not as many magically believe, that power is in no way transmitted to us by the therapist or healer.

However that force can be blocked and must be re-activated when its free flow has been impaired by trauma, guilt, fear and feelings of worthlessness, with one word: by *depression*.

I called it self-power because it's part of our higher self, and because we own it individually. And I call it primary power because it's a primal asset we bear with us since eternity.

With that power in an intact condition, we are one energetic whole, non-fragmented, holy. That also implies that we are free of codependent sucking bonds so that our bioenergetic flow is not fed into another organism where it vanishes away.

All codependence can be seen under this energetic perspective, as I have shown in more detail in more specific publications. You cannot be centered when your bioenergy is sucked away by a codependent parasite human or domestic animal.

However, many people in international consumer culture nurture such relationships in order to flee the rampant loneliness that international culture has created through the destruction of the extended family and the isolation of the elder, and generally the age-group segregation or ageism that is today part and parcel of social life in technologically developed countries.

Fusion therefore means not only lacking clarity and confusion about the I-AM force in us, but it also means a long-term exhaustion of the vital energies of at least one partner in the codependent relation.

To repeat it and to avoid misunderstandings: I do not speak here about the primary fusion of mother with newborn baby, but about what I call 'secondary fusion,' which is a search for mutual dependency that exactly sets in when the child has already reached, or should have reached, a more outgoing life and autonomy.

In addition, this secondary fusion or codependence is more often to find in mother-child relationships that were not sufficiently close and symbiotic at a time when they had to be, that is, during the first eighteen months of the baby's life.

This is the paradox that we encounter here and that makes the matter so alien for most people: it's typically the mother who suffers herself from codependence with a parent that tends to neglect to fully nurture the newborn, physically and in any other way. It's the mother that later does not want to let go the young man who, when he was a baby, was disgusted at the idea to take that baby at her breast and feed it or let it suck her nipples for the sheer oral pleasure the baby derives from it. It's the mother that later asks her young boy to dedicate himself for her that was unable to care in the first place for that fragile newborn with its exorbitant narcissistic needs. Of course, her own narcissism was clashing with that of the baby and she was disgusted at that little yucky thing being so selfish 'n naughty all the time!

This was in a forensic case I came across the lapidary statement of a mother who, after repeated hyper-violent beatings, finally gave her baby the death blow.

A sadistic narcissist reacts with violence and stress at the natural narcissism of a baby where a natural parent smiles and tries to liberate all reserves of latitude and patience he or she can mobilize. That's what childcare means, in fact, or what else?

Respectful child rearing is unthinkable without granting the child a gradually growing amount of autonomy. This is what builds self-power in the child, it's respect combined with autonomy. Self-power is natural force but it needs to be nurtured to grow undisturbed. We can also say that it's the power of the mindbody unit of the growing life. It can be observed in the free play of the child's emotions, their strong will, their fantasy, their spontaneity and a certain natural authority that children display who grow under the loving embrace of respectful parents.

This natural authority of the child, and their sometimes astonishing wisdom are directly connected to the child's soul power, their deepest intuition, their Tao. Through this authority the child distinguishes himself or herself as a self-defined person, a person who intuitively knows about her boundaries. This is a will that is fed by intuition and that says: 'I want this. I do not want that. I love this, but that I do not love.'

Life does not only want to be but it wants to be in a specific way, it wants to distinguish and re-define itself constantly, like a well-to-do business does. It wants to say: Here is I-AM and this over there is NOT I-AM. Growth, as I tried to demonstrate earlier in this study, invariably is dependent upon distinction from the matrix as its primal yet highly temporary condition: Here is I-AM and that matrix over there is NO MORE I-AM.

This objective necessity to grow away from the womb and toward the world corresponds subjectively to something like a *will for distinction* that is inherent in every growing life and that is participating in the creation of an autonomous and self-contained energy system that is clearly separated from that of the mother. It is for this reason that all and everything that disturbs the autonomy quest of the child has a direct negative impact upon the child's growth, and even daily matters such as toilet behavior, appetite, sleeping habits, psychosomatic ailments, and so forth.

A new alternative educational paradigm that is enriched by the insights from *Emonics* can only be natural, ecological and holistic for there is no question to impact in any way upon the child's energy system and its coherent mindbody continuum, but the right approach is one of restraint and respect: we only have to let nature do its job and the natural wholeness of the child display and develop all its rich foliage.

—See Peter Fritz Walter, The Energy Nature of Human Emotions and Sexual Attraction: A Systemic Analysis of

Emotional Identity in the Process of the Human Sexual Response (2015/2017).

To achieve this, one thing is of paramount importance: to respect and foster the child's natural autonomy and wistful authority by a permissive and tolerant educational approach that avoids all extremes and keeps the middle way between them.

In tribal cultures, be they of Asian, African or Caucasian origin, this knowledge is by no means new but belongs to the orally transmitted cultural heritage.

In German we call it *Volksweisheit*, which means something like the wisdom of the people, while the ambiguous English expression 'folk wisdom' not quite matches the wholly positive meaning of the German expression. It is the knowledge of grounded peoples and individuals, who not only know the laws of life but also respect these laws by living in holy communion with the earth.

Only we other postmodern city-dwellers, that we have lost most of our roots with earth must hear these truths again and again, not to learn them, but in order to rediscover them in our own intuitive consciousness and identify them as knowledge of the soul. For truth cannot be lost. It can only be veiled or hidden under cultural garbage that belongs to the first phase of industrialization and should be removed by today.

The really intricate problem is that of power abuse in relationships as a direct result of secondary fusion, the unhealthy codependence between parents and their children within the nuclear family. It's a growing problem, a problem that traces greater and greater publicity and affects greater and greater circles of people, and more and more young people especially.

After now twenty years of research into this complex of problems, I can clearly affirm that substance abuse, alcoholism, youth delinquency, incest, child abuse, child murder and even right-wing fascism, structural and collective violence, war, civil war, ethnic massacres and genocide are all to be traced back to a problem that on first sight looks rather harmless: secondary fusion.

Seen from the myths of old India, we presently live through the so-called *Kali Yuga*, the era of the Hindu goddess Kali, a negative mother imago, and this could indicate that the destructiveness of our present epoch, the abhorrent domestic violence, the massacres, the tortures, the terror attacks, the mass murders, all are to be traced back to a black matrix, a highly threatening castrating mother imago that is flooding the collective unconscious, creating something like a collective psychosis in the human master mind. I know that I can barely verify this hypothesis with the psychological or scientific tools that I have at my disposition, but there are many indications for the probability of my hypothesis. I will not bother further with it because it's not immediately impacting upon the results of this study.

Instead I will put the focus on therapeutic aspects and show ways out of the trap of secondary fusion or codependence.

It is essential to realize that any archetype as part of the individual or collective unconscious can only flood the whole of consciousness and thus dominate the individual or collective psyche if the person, or the collective of people, are not conscious of it. In the very moment wake consciousness knows about the existence of the archetype, it loses its frightening and destructive psychic energy. This energy contained in the archetype changes polarity through the laser beam of consciousness penetrating it. This energy, that was negative (yin or minus) as long as it was unconscious then changes to a positive polarity (yang or plus) and will be added-on to the whole of consciousness. This can in some cases lead to a quantum jump of the person on another sphere of consciousness in the sense of a major spiritual advancement, and in any other case will contribute to a sharper insight in the psychological workings of life and human togetherness.

This is clearly an alchemical process; consciousness has a catalyzing function: it impacts on our smaller human mind so as to open it larger toward the all-encompassing and totally conscious cosmic mind.

This transformation of individual consciousness through a catalyzing impact of collective consciousness upon it results in a stronger comprehensiveness regarding the complexity of living that the enlightened individual benefits from.

With each such transformation of individual consciousness, then, a particle of collective consciousness is transformed or reformed as well. Greater clarity, lasting freedom, enhanced vigilance and purity in love are the worldwide results of such a broadening of planetary consciousness.

On the individual level, to repeat it, every therapeutic approach starts with a sort of cleansing: to free the psyche from energetic blockages, among which hypnotic injunctions play a major role, as Transactional Analysis (TA) has clearly demonstrated since now around five decades. It is these magic spells, thrown by parents toward their children that are interfering negatively with the child's developing autonomy. The therapeutic goal here is primarily the restoration of a free flow of psychic energy in the psyche of the child or adolescent.

Regarding the complex problem of codependence, this means that the child therapist must activate the self-healing power of the child patient, and thus trigger the self-power of the person. All healing processes are effected by the patient's own genuine body energy and not in any way by a magic energy transmission from the healer toward the patient's energy system. This statement is valid even for medication-based interventions because all good medications in last resort but activate and stimulate the self-healing processes in the patient's organism.

Every therapy is self-therapy with the therapist as the catalyzing agent. Also hypnosis treatment makes no exception from this rule because every hypnosis is auto-hypnosis as Milton H. Erickson has demonstrated by his whole life's work as one of the most successful and influential hypnotic healers mankind has produced until today.

—See Milton H. Erickson, Complete Works 1.0, CD-ROM (2001) and Sydney Rosen, My Voice Will Go With You: The Teaching Tales of Milton H. Erickson (1991).

Formulating a multi-disciplinary approach for effective post-abuse treatment—and only such a wide approach will be able to deal with the high complexity of the issue—I today see one point of central importance: direct work on the emotions of the patient in a way to help the patient express them.

This sounds very easy in principle but is not in practice, because not the therapist but the patient himself or herself has to grant their organism the permission to express emotions that, perhaps almost for a lifetime, this same organism has effectively repressed. This is the crux. This permission cannot be given by the therapist *in loco patientis*. And the further crux is that the patient must reach their subconscious level because the conditioning spells are contained here, and not in wake consciousness. This is practically only achievable for a highly spiritual individual and the repeated use of meditation, while for an ordinary individual it's possibly not achievable without hypnosis and learning, from the hypnotherapist, the methods of inducing autohypnosis.

Self-hypnosis is the method that I myself learnt to practice, during my two years of hypnotherapy done fifteen years ago, and which helped me to handle my highly turbulent and confused sexuality, acute anxieties, constant depression and suicidal tendencies. At the beginning of the therapy, during one of the first hypnotherapy sessions, I have indeed given the express permission to my subconscious to let me grow into a higher level of autonomy, consciousness and personal power! My very wistful psychotherapist knew that this was the primary condition for my progress. He knew because he had been a direct student with Milton Erickson in his years of learning in the United States. After this first step that opens something like a gateway or might prepare a possible quantum jump later on, comes the usual, and more well-known, intellectual and linguistic work that serves to humanize all our emotions.

Emotions are our antennas for self-feeling: sensing the whole of our body, without leaving parts out, equates sensing our whole being. Here we practically experience the intricate connection between body and mind. To feel yourself then becomes feeling being yourself, and in last resort feeling your self in the sense of realizing your spiritual unity with the whole of the universe. This is achieved through recognizing all your emotions as unconditionally yours.

Only through recognizing our emotions we can eventually realize our wholeness. And as, according to Ramana Maharshi and other sages, we have never lost this wholeness, but only are confused about it, we can develop the strong conviction that we are healed-and-whole again which in itself is the most powerful motor for complete renewal on all levels of the self, and also on the behavior level.

Let me clarify what sounds like a contradiction. I really have to stress here the notion of the ego that is shunned so much in spiritual literature and also in more recent psychological publications. What is that dirty ego good for?

—See Peter Fritz Walter, The Ego Matter: About the Importance of Autonomy for Realizing Your True Self, Scholarly Articles, Vol. 7 (2015/2017).

The first thing I want to say is that it's nothing dirty at all, but something highly useful because if you had no ego you would be psychotic. It's as simple as that. So it's not done with traveling to India and throwing your ego overboard that you will make any kind of real progress on the spiritual path. Forget the alluring reports by others, they are all wrong or cunningly invented for money-making.

It's amazing how many highly intelligent Westerners are lured into the dangerous labyrinth of voluntary psychosis by sly experts of spiritual business on both hemispheres of the globe. For spiritual progress you need not no ego but in the contrary a very strong and highly structured ego. The misunderstanding is created by contemporary folk wisdom that makes us believe an adamant ego was leading to egocentrism and selfishness.

Rather the contrary is true. A strong ego is the condition for the quantum leap that leads to surpassing the ego. There is no other way.

The ego must be transformed through its inherent self-power, through its own cunning intelligence that ultimately leads to the dissolution of the ego. When I was developing this insight around fifteen years ago, I could not believe it at first and tried to find evidence to corroborate it. So I examined the numerological themes of quite a number of sages, among them on the first places of the list Buddha, Aurobindo, Krishnamurti and Maharshi. And I found that they had extremely strong ego's. And don't think I confused ego with self. I am talking about the ego, not about the self. I am talking about self-centeredness and even pride. Everyone who has seen K (Krishnamurti) on video and tells me that this man had not an unwavering natural pride, and a strong one, is a day-dreamer or just believes every joke he is told. Aurobindo and Gurdjieff were reported to have been high-strung at times, and firm and stout also toward authorities, be it the highest in the country or in the world.

A strong ego cannot develop when there is codependence. In this constellation, typically, one ego is coupled with another ego and for both the development of genuine individuality and autonomy is impaired as long as the codependence lasts. To have one's focus entirely upon one's own life and destiny is not at all selfishness, nor self-centeredness in a bad sense, but a very healthy psychic condition!

We can only develop sensitivity for others and the earth as a whole when we have integrated our ego, not by denying it. Integrating our ego means first of all accepting its existence. This is, then, the right evolutionary direction to give to yourself: be self-centered and accept your ego.

Attention: I did not say be ego-centered. This is the fundamental difference while terminologically the two alternatives sound very similar!

Surpassing your ego? You can only surpass what exists, what you have built beforehand. You cannot surpass a non-existent ego that resides in an otherwise psychotic mind. Without ego your mind is invaded by all and everything, without having boundaries. That's not very agreeable, not even temporarily.

How you are going to live with total perception without your mind exploding or you jumping out of the window?

It's very dangerous, really, to engage in sudden mind-opening experiences without an expert guide at your side, and many end in psychiatric hospitals after their so-called spiritual journeys.

Tell me what is spiritual in such foolish endeavors? Is preparing a bowl of soup not something spiritual? Is taking care of your child not something spiritual? Is having fantastic and happy sex not something spiritual? Why the hell do you need to travel to India in order to feel spiritual …? It's but a fashion and it will vanish as sudden as it began.

And there you are again, back home, tendering your garden, pampering your children, feeding your pets, sweeping the floor and cooking your soup. And have you got rid of your ego? Did your guru buy it from you? If you are at all serious, stop all this nonsense and begin doing your home work.

Your home work begins at home, and it ends at home. It begins with yourself and it ends with yourself. And not in India. And not on the moon. You want to experience psychosis? Go ahead, but I promise you that you will return home anyway. And nothing will have changed besides you got your six senses back, and stay with same old soup.

What many preachers of consciousness boosting have overlooked is that you can enlarge only what before has been compressed. That's not my insight, but Lao-tzu said this, quite some time ago, in his *Tao Te Ching*. If you want to blow up your ego, you have to strengthen it first, and a lot! How to do that? By getting to know it. What is it all about? Is it yellow or is it red, big or small, smooth or hairy?

It's neither of this, of course. But you can find out by yourself instead of running to the next guru. You can begin to be your own guru, simply by studying the nature of your ego.

Realizing your wholeness can only be brought about through self-knowledge. It's knowledge about the whole of your mindbody continuum, and thus knowledge about your conscious and subconscious processes, physically, mentally and emotionally, including your dreams. It also means to become aware of the kaleidoscopic play and function of your emotions by passively observing and accepting them.

Let me deal with another widespread misunderstanding. I always remember a university colleague telling me this in a law class:

—You know, my girlfriend is really craving for me now. I have educated her that way so that she participates in really swinish sex and obeys me in every respect. But now the game takes a different turn. She is now so terribly hot for me that she does not give me any more rest. And now I want to get rid of her again because she somehow has become a baby girl clinging to her all-powerful father. This disgusts me to a point that I will throw her out at the next occasion.

Healing codependent relationships, for example with your partner, close friends or your concubine generally does not come about by just cutting these bonds. In the contrary do such brutal reactions signal that there is a high anxiety regarding separation. Cutting the bond will not bring any change. One dummy partner will be replaced by another. And we are home in the same bed again. And wake up with the same bad taste in our mouth. So far so good. What then?

Codependence can only be tackled from inside, not from outside, from within the body, not from without the body, within yourself and without even involving your fusional partner in any way. For the problem is not your partner, but you. To say it in a somewhat extreme manner: you are caught in an illusion.

When the umbilical bond was cut that connected you with the organism of your mother, your body was autonomous. You may object: true, but not my mind. That's correct. The metaphoric umbilical bond, that we are talking about here, is a creation of the psyche. But this illusion, as long as it is not recognized as such, and as Carl Jung has shown us with strong evidence, is reality. Unconscious thought will trigger action and experience, so that we incarnate this subconscious content of consciousness into daily reality.

Encountering your fear of separation will lead you to over-react and harshly cut off the bond that you first sanctified and then sent to hell. This is of course a paradoxical behavior but psychologically sound. You run away. And after a few days the tension is so high that you find another puppet-partner. 'This love is going to be the total one, so total in fact that you will absorb her into yourself and there will be no more discussions.' Yes, if all was as easy as that …

Frequent partner change is the result of codependence. You search it out and you flee it. This is the paradox of it all. You copulate but you are not close to each other. You do not meet, while you may pass a lot of time in bed together. You flee it again, and you replace it with another scenario that repeats the same show. And so on and so forth. Every time you hope it will be different and you will be disappointed, realizing that it's same old soup every time. The same short moment of excitement and the long moments of boredom thereafter.

You experience fear as a matter of logic: your codependent relationship is much closer to a parent-child relation than to a partner relation, and thus invokes in you memories of your childhood. But these memories are the last things you need in your adult life, right? When you remember, your pain comes back, your pain of never having realized autonomy in your childhood and having been the cute puppet for one of your parents! You are afraid to experience more frustration, you fear that this depression tears you down again into the gutter of loneliness, and of negativism, in that condition where you only want one thing: fall asleep and never wake up again to the same life!

The crux of codependence is that you cannot only experience the positive part of it without cashing in the negative part. And the negative part is exactly the upsurge of your early anxieties, your ongoing childhood depression, your rage and your many frustrations in seeking emotional and sexual fulfillment in a really fulfilling partner relation.

I know and I am not making fun of you. I went through all that myself, and really the hard way, with all that it involves, including social downfall, divorce and disgust with adult females for more than a decade to follow.

When you are codependent you are on the loser track, do what you will, because you get the sweetness of love only poisoned by a gall-bitter pill in the very center of it.

Of course, from a perspective of common sense, all this is hardly intelligent behavior, but that's not the point, absolutely not. The point is that it's inevitable and you have to go through it because you can't go around it. Same like with that thing you want to expand and that first you need to compress, or with surpassing your ego. See it?

All observation of nature and its laws shows us that for any kind of evolution, personal or collective, we need to get rid of old skins, just like serpents do.

What would be the condition of a butterfly was it forced to still bear the heavy shell of the larva? Could it fly around so graciously or would it rather look like a clumsy idiot-butterfly? Or imagine your adult body was still wrapped in the skin you had as a baby. This skin has not stretched to the size of your present body, but has been renewed, and was completely changed.

Our body replaces its skin every eleven months! Entirely. Thus, every year we virtually have a new body!

When the flow of vital energies is normal and there is no neurosis or psychosis, our emotional life can well be compared with leaving behind old skins. It's a constant death and rebirth, a steady flow like the tidings of the ocean. And our self-healing power is dependent upon the free flow of our emotions and their inherent bioenergetic flow.

But this is fully possible only in closed, not in open energy systems. Codependence creates a leaking valve in your flow system where the energy is streaming out of your system. While you need a closed flow system so that the energy remains within your own mindbody continuum, building up enough momentum for your next quantum leap. That is why, seen energetically, codependent couples experience as good as no personal evolution.

I went through it myself, during seventeen years of a completely codependent marriage that remained infertile in every meaning of the word.

Only in fully separated flow systems it's possible to counter entropy and to pent up and save a certain amount of energy not needed for daily working and living. In fusionally coupled energy systems, this is not possible. What happens is that one system is emptied and the other flows over. But the energy receiver usually cannot use the received energy creatively and thus wastes it either through obsessive sexuality or through vanity endeavors, instead of taking care of self-development and evolution.

What this boils down to is a fundamental imbalance of the two energy systems in relation to each other.

Harmony is only possible in a relationship where both partners, and related energy systems, swing together in a sort of pendulum movement. This is ideally also the case in the healthy relationship between mother and newborn. But in this case only because the newborn has not yet developed a separated ego.

This is also the normal condition in the plant world where there are many highly effective symbiotic relationships to be found. This is so because plants do not have an ego and do not need one. They are naturally psychotic.

Plants also can allow other beings talk through them. Plant consciousness is structured differently than animal/human consciousness; it is broader, and much more symbiotic, but it can hardly serve as example for solving our codependence problems. We must begin with what we have got: we have got an ego, and thus have to begin with that.

It is easy to understand that codependence always is a first step toward schizophrenia. Or, to formulate it positively, and in accordance with the founders of antipsychiatry, Thomas Szasz and Ronald David Laing: at the origin of schizophrenia is but an extreme amount of lacking autonomy, a problem of especially stringent codependence that develops in a malign manner.

Let me stop here and summarize: in all codependence is involved one dominating and one subordinating ego. Now, from these cases we have to distinguish the relations where there is not subordination, but equality.

We all remember our childhood friendships, relationships where there was no subordination but equality. They typically were same-sex relations, and they were exceptional in that all was shared except one's skin: feelings, blood, saliva, hair, sperm, secrets, clothes, shoes, experiences, and more. Often also love relations are shared. But anyway if not the love partner is herself shared, the story is shared, up until its most intimate details.

Among adolescents, cofusion is sought after with delight and, if possible, is enjoyed sexually in all its dimensions. This may also be transported into adulthood and is in many cases. It means that the first girlfriend might be shared as well … as long and as far as she participates.

While case stories naturally differ, youth friendships bear amazing similarities, as if they all magically fell into one pattern. But it's relatively seldom that one child really dominates another. This constellation exists, for example in the case that a young boy has internalized his cannibalistic mother and projects her inversely upon his little friend, and here often a smaller child is sought out as a fusion-partner, in order to act out one's own oral fixation with changed roles.

The small boy is going to get the same treatment as oneself got from big mum, the same beatings, the same love bites, the same ferocious mix between love and hate that can drive the little one into real trauma.

And from the perspective of the smaller child, things make sense as well. He has sought another totally possessive mother and found it in the person of his adolescent fusion-partner, and unconsciously in order to heal that problematic relationship with his own mother.

That I'm not talking about theory here knows everybody who, like me, has passed his whole childhood in homes, from age two to eighteen, or who has read more or less famous literary accounts of them, such as, for example 'Der junge Törless' by the German author Siegfried Lenz, a novel that has been used as a script for a very successful film with the same title, or 'Les amitiés particulières' by Roger Peyrefitte, a novel that equally made a very popular film.

My point is that, contrary to codependence, fusional youth relations exert a healing effect and are actually dissolving codependence that is experienced with parents or siblings.

These relationships between children and adolescents, contrary to the brutal treatment and utter violence they receive in the United States are completely natural. There is nothing parents or caretakers have to worry about. It is Oedipal Culture's madness to qualify them as abusive in relation of the older toward the younger child and even incarcerate adolescents for so-called child abuse, as this is currently practiced in the United States.

Let me cite here also the blood friendships among North American Indians that resemble a bit our ado-friendships, but are held between adults. Here we see that it's well possible that fusional bonds do not need to be codependent, but that fusion between humans is possible like symbiosis among plants.

It is without any doubt that blood friendships among natives are closed on the basis of mutual autonomy, and only among adults who have reached autonomy.

Natives assign fusional friendships between children a different value than those between adults. Without belittling children bonds, they regard blood friendship among adult male warriors as the highest form of friendship.

It seems that real intimacy can only be based upon full autonomy of both partners in the relationship. In these rituals, where a little quantity of blood is symbolically exchanged or other fusional gestures are given to seal the bond of the two souls, we are not talking about secondary fusion, but about authentic friendship.

What I wish to show in the present study is not so much the pathological aspects of what I call emotional incest, because those were studied already, however without the collective dimension that I am going to discuss in the last chapter of the booklet.

What I am curious about, instead, is to find out how and under which conditions fusional friendship, also between generations, can be therapeutic in a wider sense of the term? This idea does not seem too far-fetched when we consider a basic law of evolution, which is that every evolution proceeds in a spiraled manner. This means namely that a specific problem or problem complex is not just dissolved when a quantum leap happens, but transported higher and higher on the evolutionary hierarchy and actually serves as the very motor of the evolution.

You can call this the principle 'Nature does not kill.' It also does not segregate or discard out the bad elements as modern society does, but uses them creatively as catalyzing agents for growth. I have seen this all my life through. My sexual attraction for children, while it has given me major trouble, was at the same time the one single most important motor of my personal evolution, until today.

All these people thrown in prisons, all these young people who are thrown in centers of special care are immensely important for society to grow, and to change. It is a collective crime to discard people out from the community only because they have not known to handle their vital energies.

Many tribal cultures have means to deal with social delinquency without discarding people out from the community, or they do it only for a very short period, such as one day. In some tribal cultures, even murderers were punished with segregation from their village for the period of exactly twenty-four hours.

You can think a lot during twenty-four hours. And you cannot think substantially more in twenty-four years!

What happens instead in our prisons is that human potential is wasted and thrown into the gutter, and no society ever can afford this to happen in the long run without damaging its very substance of existence and evolution!

What exactly happens in the evolutionary cycle is that the primary event, let's say the missed symbiosis between mother and newborn, will be put on stage as a projection time and again. But each time the protagonists of the play have a higher level of consciousness. The chance to eventually heal the original conflict are thus higher with each new cycle of evolution. And that love is the best of all therapies, I do not need to repeat here. We all know it.

But who really uses this knowledge in their own life or even directs their life from this insight? There are so many deep insights in simple people, and in old people, that we could use as a society, and that we yet totally disregard.

Why is that so? Why have we, or the generations before us, allowed it to happen that love was soiled and became a subject of suspicion and fear since the early beginnings of patriarchy?

The answer is simple. Love has not been recognized as what it is, and this is a typical outcome of the blindness and deafness of the patriarchal view of the world.

Many of us believe or have been conditioned to believe love was a sort of unhealthy attachment, while they don't understand that true love is the exact contrary of secondary fusion and actually dissolves codependence.

Love is freedom. Love can exist only where free hearts meet and where both partners are autonomous beings that swing, each, in their own energetic balance. Love is magic in the sense that it sweeps all that not really belongs to it, and thus can clean out hearts from a lot of clutter. Love can help us remove sub-cultural garbage from our minds and hearts.

To explain this in energetic terms, we can say that through opening the heart chakra the bioenergy that became stuck and retrograde during the missed oedipal development, can again swing back into its natural state of dynamic balance. Thus, the energetic flow that was stuck is moving again.

No criminal law can regulate love. Such laws are truly criminal. The same is true for all those laws that, as it is called, are protecting minors. These laws are still more criminal in that they enslave the child instead of helping the child to experience love in all its dimensions and thus be put on a path of dynamic evolution.

Not moralism will help us solve our current social problems, but an ethic that again puts love on the first place, as it was in all peaceful and wistful tribal cultures.

I have called this the love principle and found it to be a universal pattern of living in all natural tribal societies.

CHAPTER THREE

The Illusion of Collective Fusion

> For I should think that it's not really agreeable to our
> rulers that there is higher insight and firm bonds
> among our subordinates, which is something that
> habitually comes about through love.
>
> —PLATO, BANQUET

The problem of *Power or Depression*, theme of this study, is that it is a cultural phenomenon that is rooted in our evolution as a human race.

As I have pointed out in the previous chapter, the main problem complex regarding depression is secondary fusion or codependence. I have explained in which points secondary fusion differs from primary fusion, the symbiotic bond we maintain with our mothers for our first eighteen months after birth.

Now I invite us to look at things more from the point of view of our imagination. What we really seek out in secondary fusion is namely linked to primary fusion on the level of our unconscious memories that surge up as more or less spontaneous mental images.

These images suggest serenity, a tranquil swinging water-bound condition in which incoming sounds are smoothed, weight is alleviated and joy comes from a silence continuum and a certain careless living into the day—because one is fed through the umbilical cord. It seems to me that the fetal condition is a very creative one, an endless orgasm in fact, for both mother and child.

These remembrances of a lost paradise are deeply carved into the bones of our subconscious mind, and they tend to be projected onto all new relationships we seek out. They are the stuff for dreams in secondary fusion as well; they make for people seeking out new fusion partners after each break. It's this fantastic imagery that pervades the unconscious like a never-ending song of love. They say: 'Let me be your baby and you will be my baby. I will feed you and you will feed me. I will carry you in my womb and you will carry me in your womb. And one day I will give you birth and you will give me birth. And we will be newborn souls in the universe—through our love.'

You hear that suggested in each and every love song. And this is logically so because it's directly flowing from our collective consciousness into all our thoughts and actions.

Now, the further step I invite you to take is to see that you can project this imagery of a lost paradise not only upon individuals, but also upon groups, organisms, political parties, sects, sport clubs or groupings that incarnate certain ideologies whatever their names are.

To demonstrate what I mean, let us first have a look at what means *integration*. What is the difference between fusion and integration? Integration is the loyal cooperation of an individual with a greater whole, a group, community, or organism.

But will you remain an individual once you are within the group or will you be dissolved into an obedient automaton? This depends on two factors:

----the strength of your individuality; and

----the nature of your integration into the organism.

The relationship between individuals and the state can be described as integration when it's a democratic state, and as fusion when it's an ant republic.

While this makes sense, it's not very precise, because if the person is not really individualized and looks for pseudo-symbiosis with the group, then the group will tend to eat the person, and thus try to put her autonomy level to zero.

Such a person can be eaten as well by a democratic organism, while a really individualized person may not at all be fusionable into a fascist grouping and instead keep her autonomy, so that we face a real form of cooperation.

Thus, to have a deeper look at this intriguing question shows that it's more on the side of the person, and less on the side of the group that we have to look. It depends mainly on the person herself, and her level of autonomy and individualization how the relationship with the group will be like: egalitarian-synergistic or subordinate-symbiotic.

With this in mind, what follows shows more the general problem and the inherent danger in fusional group-individual relationship, while we always might suppose that a strong individualized person can resist being eaten by an organism.

Here we can also observe the behavior of nation states for there we also encounter pseudosymbiotic problems, either through territorial invasion as an attempt of fusion or through defending such invasion, that is, the defense of fusion.

Why did I entitle this chapter as illusion of collective fusion? The stress is well on *illusion*.

Fusion is an illusion where the individual is eaten. When we look at symbiosis in nature we always see that both plants continue living and growing and profit from the symbiosis, and that not one plant eats the other and gets a one-sided profit.

An organism that defends the individual from exhibiting their own creative contribution or annihilates any autonomous contribution of the individual is a machine that needs wheels, not humans.

Individuals in the turning wheel of a machinery may nominally exhibit high productivity but, seen from a point of view of human evolution, such an ant republic is a zero endeavor in terms of personal growth, or it even retrogrades the human potential.

I speak of illusion because seen from an outside level, we often do not see the truth about the destruction of humanity by such fascist, revolutionary or terrorist organisms; what we only see is a certain productivity that we judge as a signal for effective human cooperation. But that is precisely the deception and the danger of such organisms.

The stagnation or retrogradation of the human potential within such organisms is veiled, is occulted.

Illusion also because many people commit the error to believe that a community endeavor runs better when all its members are really fusioned into it and have thus more or less abandoned the distance they naturally maintained when they were still individuals.

I have seen this happen with a friend who became member of a religious sect or church; after around two weeks of brainwashing he was completely turned around, another person than the one I had known before. It was frightening. But I must say that after having observed him for two years before that happened, I was aware that he had a very weak ego, was oscillating greatly in his endeavors and relationships, indiscriminate about his sexual partners and had absolutely no perspective for his future.

He had given up a very prospering PHD project and teaching post in the United States only to return to France where he installed himself in the garage of his mother's house with the fancy idea to become a painter. And it was there where it happened, when, so lost in his shaky lifestyle, dependent on drugs and alcohol and any kind of sex for killing his boredom, he encountered, through a friend's invitation, the people of that church.

And they were cunning enough to not reveal their sordid program to him right away. They were eating him slowly and thoroughly, bit by bit, but without leaving one bite for the dogs.

His letters that formerly were literary productions of high lucidity and emotionality become pamphlets with pages and pages of Bible references, exhortations, admonitions. I let it go for about six months, always hoping he could find the force to turn away from these black-coated pigs, but he was unable to, and I broke off the relationship.

To believe that any form of collective endeavor could improve the human condition is one of the greatest errors of mankind. The human is perfect as an individual and through synergistic cooperation with other individuals good results can be achieved, but to believe that the togetherness with other humans could improve the human potential is an absolutely deceptive belief.

When we study what the greatest sages of mankind say and always said, it's rather through solitary study and comfortable aloneness (not loneliness) that the human develops all that makes him surpass himself in the long run. The greatest evolutionary potential is rooted in the single human, not in the group human, in solitary life and not in group life, and also not forcibly in family life.

All totalitarian ideologies and systems and their protagonists define the family as an oedipal breeding machine and use codependence in education so as to bring about weak and confused humans, because truly individuated and autonomous beings are much more difficult to control and to manipulate. This is done through youth organizations such as the *Hitlerjugend*, the Nazi youth organization and similar organisms in more recent times, and inter alia through gender segregation, strict education with brutal forms of punishment, codependent relationships between educators and youth, and the integration of family, youth organizations and the military for propagandistic reasons. In order to avoid the development of intimate relationships between the young, each member of the organization, adult or child, is supposed to ruthlessly spy out and denunciate any suspect intimate behavior and report it to the caporal.

Such systems, because of their denial of any true humanity cannot last. The human machine cannot run smoothly and naturally on violence and draconian laws. What such systems produce is chaos and they destroy the human potential in the long run. The laws of nature are opposing such systems since they are fundamentally directed against nature.

Nothing can in the long run be reached on a collective level if not all participants contribute from a genuine will and integrity to build something greater than personal. When a system is cruel, no human is in the long run willed to maintain being motivated, and integrity vanishes. All fascists, be they right-wing or leftist, are blind to the fact that restricting the human potential through dogmatism and cruelty cannot produce anything but chaos and sad mediocrity.

Whoso reigns without the human reigns without life. And he will built a dead regime from the start. It is not important how we qualify the relationship between the individual and the collective, if we call it with Rousseau and Locke social contract or citizenship, it must be organized in a democratic way the preserves the fundamental freedom and civil rights of the individual and that is set to integrate humans rather than eat them through fusion.

Education, therefore, must be directed toward the development of individual creativity, and not toward group productivity. As fascism shuns the creative and integrative cooperation of the individual, it's a very unproductive ideology. What it brings about, and has brought about historically, is collective crime, not heroic humanity which it however pretends to foster by paying lip service to great ideals and pretendedly selfless leaders.

I would go as far as saying that truly integrative and respectful relationships between individuals and groups, or the state, can be true love relations. This sounds a bit sentimental, but a deeper regard upon Japanese culture and company life teaches us a very interesting and I think important lesson in this respect.

Where the system truly respects the individual and fosters personal growth, the individual, in turn, is highly motivated to sustain the system in times of crisis, and, for example, will work without salary when the company is passing a critical downward spiral.

When companies, as it is in Japan, do not set off their workers when they reach the end of their work cycle, and continue to pay salaries, workers will give to their company their full integrative support. When there is honesty and cooperation between superiors and inferiors, says the I Ching, the state prospers.

The Japanese system may have instituted true and beneficial symbiosis between the individual and commercial companies, be they multinationals, where the individual is respected in their full integrity as a person and as a citizen.

This system could thus be cited as one of the rare exceptions to the rule that usually such relationships end up in collective fusion.

Where the more powerful does not use his power over the less powerful, but practices self-restraint, his power becomes greater at the inside level, says the I Ching in hexagram thirty-four.

And in the long run it's this inside power that brings about revolutionary changes in human conduct and animates people to surpass themselves without being forced to. While secondary powers always bring about worldly effects such as dominance, power hunger and the reign of the fittest, primary power respects the individual and brings about personal growth.

When a system is able to respect and integrate the full individual, it benefits in multiple ways because the individual will give a surplus of creativity and originality to the system, a surplus that sometimes brings about miracles.

When the individual is respected by the system and fostered in their personal development and education, he or she will give the system in return a value that per se cannot be measured, because it is immense.

There is no greater power than human creativeness and integrity.

Where the collective grants the individual the chance to realize his or her unique potential, this will be positively reflected within the system, and the input that returns from the individual toward the system will not be twofold, but thousandfold.

Loyalty and integrity are values that have no value, that cannot be paid, that cannot be bought, and that cannot be bought and that cannot be brought about by force and cruelty. This is the true reason why the egalitarian-democratic societal system per se is the most creative, the most productive and the one that best uses the human potential.

From the foregoing follows that the criteria I have developed to distinguish love from dependency can also be used for finding out the truth about organizations, and even about the nature of political regimes. Beyond that, they help us understand the behavior of nation states.

Public international law indeed is a modern version of the antique *law of courtesy* that reigned among principles such as kings, dukes, barons, and other rulers in the definition of international law. For our present relationships between nation states, as they are part of a modernized vintage of international law, no other principles can be applied.

States behave in pretty much the same way as individuals do. Pseudo-fusion in international law, as I mentioned already earlier, can be identified by a precise vocabulary that is worldwide part of international law.

In original French language, in which international law was first drafted, when a country invaded another, the term was *envahissement*. And in psychology, in French, we talk about 'une mère envahissante,' that is a hyper-possessive, narcissistic and cannibalistic mother. Further, we talk about protectorates in international law which are regions of one country that are under the protection of another country and that are, as we all know, exploited by that other country.

And in psychology we speak of over-protective or codependent parents, implying that they exploit the child by behaving like vampires and gradually suck the child empty of vital energy.

Finally, international law speaks of the fusion of two states or regions thereof, and of separation, just as we do in psychology when we speak about relationships.

But not only in the political and international sphere but also in the religious world we encounter fusional demands of the collective, in the form of churches toward individuals called 'believers.'

This has nothing to do with true religion but always was a question of religious establishment seeking power over people. Let me cite only Krishnamurti and Maharshi as the main exponents of the view that religion is primarily a private matter and that all organized religion destroys true and authentic religious feelings.

In addition, it is easy to see that no organization can tell you what your truth is and which spiritual path is yours, as there are so many.

Recognizing truth is not an intellectual endeavor, but the art of living with what is essential and discarding out what is not. It is not any transcendental value, but acceptance of daily reality so as to transform it to a joyful continuum that is embraced by your soul.

POSTFACE

The Path of Individual Liberation

Before you can recognize truth, you need to have acquired freedom. There is no truth without freedom. What does that mean?

It does not mean to believe anything. It's rather a condition where there are no more beliefs, but moment-to-moment awareness.

To get there, most of us, especially Westerners, will combine a process of intellectual insight with some or the other psychosomatic work on the body, such as Yoga, Tao Yoga, Tai Chi or martial arts such as Zen archery.

And, not to forget of course, it is essential to work on your liberation from codependence and to build autonomy and personal identity; you do this by integrating your emotions and by realizing primary power. All this serves to develop your consciousness. Illumination is nothing but an evolution of consciousness.

The realization of freedom must deal with our voluntary and involuntary dependencies, and heal depression.

In Eastern spiritual literature, this complex of problems is generally discussed under a different, more general, header. The condition that I simply call love is described differently by believing Christians, Muslims, Hindus or Buddhists.

The dichotomies love-dependence and power-depression are discussed in Hindu religious literature in terms of egolessness versus selfishness.

The traditional terminology seems to be wider and more general: he who is enclosed in his ego without contact to his authentic self must deal not only with the problem of power but also with materialism.

What is seldom expressly said in religious literature is that love by itself brings about liberation.

If you are serious with walking the path of love, you surely don't need religion! Because love is religion, and at the same time beyond religion.

BIBLIOGRAPHY

Contextual Bibliography

Ariès, Philippe

Centuries of Childhood
New York: Vintage Books, 1962

Arntz, William & Chasse, Betsy

What the Bleep Do We Know
20th Century Fox, 2005 (DVD)

Down The Rabbit Hole Quantum Edition
20th Century Fox, 2006 (3 DVD Set)

Covitz, Joel

Emotional Child Abuse
The Family Curse
Boston: Sigo Press, 1986

DeMause, Lloyd

The History of Childhood
New York, 1974

Foundations of Psychohistory
New York: Creative Roots, 1982

Diamond, Stephen A., May, Rollo

Anger, Madness, and the Daimonic
The Psychological Genesis of Violence, Evil and Creativity
New York: State University of New York Press, 1999

DiCarlo, Russell E. (Ed.)

Towards A New World View
Conversations at the Leading Edge
Erie, PA: Epic Publishing, 1996

Dolto, Françoise

La Cause des Enfants
Paris: Laffont, 1985

Psychanalyse et Pédiatrie
Paris: Seuil, 1971

Séminaire de Psychanalyse d'Enfants, 1
Paris: Seuil, 1982

Séminaire de Psychanalyse d'Enfants, 2
PARIS: SEUIL, 1985

Séminaire de Psychanalyse d'Enfants, 3
PARIS: SEUIL, 1988

L'évangile au risque de la psychanalyse
PARIS: SEUIL, 1980

EISLER, RIANE

The Chalice and the Blade
OUR HISTORY, OUR FUTURE
SAN FRANCISCO: HARPER & ROW, 1995

Sacred Pleasure: Sex, Myth and the Politics of the Body
NEW PATHS TO POWER AND LOVE
SAN FRANCISCO: HARPER & ROW, 1996

The Partnership Way
NEW TOOLS FOR LIVING AND LEARNING
WITH DAVID LOYE
BRANDON, VT: HOLISTIC EDUCATION PRESS, 1998

The Real Wealth of Nations
CREATING A CARING ECONOMICS
SAN FRANCISCO: BERRETT-KOEHLER PUBLISHERS, 2008

ELLIS, HAVELOCK

Sexual Inversion
REPUBLISHED
NEW YORK: UNIVERSITY PRESS OF THE PACIFIC, 2001
ORIGINALLY PUBLISHED IN 1897

The Sexual Impulse in Women
REPUBLISHED
NEW YORK: UNIVERSITY PRESS OF THE PACIFIC, 2001
ORIGINALLY PUBLISHED IN 1903

The Dance of Life
NEW YORK: GREENWOOD PRESS REPRINT EDITION, 1973
ORIGINALLY PUBLISHED IN 1923

ELWIN, V.

The Muria and their Ghotul
BOMBAY: OXFORD UNIVERSITY PRESS, 1947

ERICKSON, MILTON H.

My Voice Will Go With You
THE TEACHING TALES OF MILTON H. ERICKSON
BY SIDNEY ROSEN (ED.)
NEW YORK: NORTON & CO., 1991

Complete Works 1.0, CD-ROM
NEW YORK: MILTON H. ERICKSON FOUNDATION, 2001

FREUD, SIGMUND

The Interpretation of Dreams
NEW YORK: AVON, REISSUE EDITION, 1980
AND IN: THE STANDARD EDITION OF THE COMPLETE PSYCHOLOGICAL
WORKS OF SIGMUND FREUD , (24 VOLUMES) ED. BY JAMES STRACHEY
NEW YORK: W. W. NORTON & COMPANY, 1976

Totem and Taboo
NEW YORK: ROUTLEDGE, 1999
ORIGINALLY PUBLISHED IN 1913

FROMM, ERICH

The Anatomy of Human Destructiveness
NEW YORK: OWL BOOK, 1992
ORIGINALLY PUBLISHED IN 1973

Escape from Freedom
NEW YORK: OWL BOOKS, 1994
ORIGINALLY PUBLISHED IN 1941
TO HAVE OR TO BE
NEW YORK: CONTINUUM INTERNATIONAL PUBLISHING, 1996
ORIGINALLY PUBLISHED IN 1976

The Art of Loving
NEW YORK: HARPERPERENNIAL, 2000
ORIGINALLY PUBLISHED IN 1956

GOLEMAN, DANIEL

Emotional Intelligence
NEW YORK, BANTAM BOOKS, 1995

GORDON, ROSEMARY

Pedophilia: Normal and Abnormal
IN: KRAEMER, THE FORBIDDEN LOVE
LONDON, 1976

GOSWAMI, AMIT

The Self-Aware Universe
HOW CONSCIOUSNESS CREATES THE MATERIAL WORLD
NEW YORK: TARCHER/PUTNAM, 1995

GROTH, A. NICHOLAS

Men Who Rape
THE PSYCHOLOGY OF THE OFFENDER
NEW YORK: PERSEUS PUBLISHING, 1980

HAMEROFF, NEWBERG, WOOLF, BIERMAN

Consciousness
20 SCIENTISTS INTERVIEWED
DIRECTOR: GREGORY ALSBURY
5 DVD BOX SET, 540 MIN.
NEW YORK: ALSBURY FILMS, 2003

JAMES, WILLIAM

Writings 1902-1910
THE VARIETIES OF RELIGIOUS EXPERIENCE / PRAGMATISM / A PLURALISTIC
UNIVERSE / THE MEANING OF TRUTH / SOME PROBLEMS OF PHILOSOPHY /
ESSAYS
NEW YORK: LIBRARY OF AMERICA, 1988

JUNG, CARL GUSTAV

Archetypes of the Collective Unconscious
IN: THE BASIC WRITINGS OF C.G. JUNG
NEW YORK: THE MODERN LIBRARY, 1959, 358-407

Collected Works
NEW YORK, 1959

On the Nature of the Psyche
IN: THE BASIC WRITINGS OF C.G. JUNG
NEW YORK: THE MODERN LIBRARY, 1959, 47-133

Psychological Types
COLLECTED WRITINGS, VOL. 6
PRINCETON: PRINCETON UNIVERSITY PRESS, 1971

Psychology and Religion
IN: THE BASIC WRITINGS OF C.G. JUNG
NEW YORK: THE MODERN LIBRARY, 1959, 582-655

Religious and Psychological Problems of Alchemy
IN: THE BASIC WRITINGS OF C.G. JUNG
NEW YORK: THE MODERN LIBRARY, 1959, 537-581

The Basic Writings of C.G. Jung
NEW YORK: THE MODERN LIBRARY, 1959

The Development of Personality
COLLECTED WRITINGS, VOL. 17
PRINCETON: PRINCETON UNIVERSITY PRESS, 1954

The Meaning and Significance of Dreams
BOSTON: SIGO PRESS, 1991

The Myth of the Divine Child
IN: ESSAYS ON A SCIENCE OF MYTHOLOGY
PRINCETON, N.J.: PRINCETON UNIVERSITY PRESS BOLLINGEN
SERIES XXII, 1969. (WITH KARL KERENYI)

Two Essays on Analytical Psychology
COLLECTED WRITINGS, VOL. 7
PRINCETON: PRINCETON UNIVERSITY PRESS, 1972
FIRST PUBLISHED BY ROUTLEDGE & KEGAN PAUL, LTD., 1953

KLEIN, MELANIE

Love, Guilt and Reparation, and Other Works 1921-1945
NEW YORK: FREE PRESS, 1984
(REISSUE EDITION)

Envy and Gratitude and Other Works 1946-1963
NEW YORK: FREE PRESS, 2002
(REISSUE EDITION)

KOESTLER, ARTHUR

The Act of Creation
NEW YORK: PENGUIN ARKANA, 1989.
ORIGINALLY PUBLISHED IN 1964

KRISHNAMURTI, J.

Freedom From The Known
SAN FRANCISCO: HARPER & ROW, 1969

The First and Last Freedom
SAN FRANCISCO: HARPER & ROW, 1975

Education and the Significance of Life
LONDON: VICTOR GOLLANCZ, 1978

BIBLIOGRAPHY

Commentaries on Living
FIRST SERIES
LONDON: VICTOR GOLLANCZ, 1985

Commentaries on Living
SECOND SERIES
LONDON: VICTOR GOLLANCZ, 1986

Krishnamurti's Journal
LONDON: VICTOR GOLLANCZ, 1987

Krishnamurti's Notebook
LONDON: VICTOR GOLLANCZ, 1986

Beyond Violence
LONDON: VICTOR GOLLANCZ, 1985

Beginnings of Learning
NEW YORK: PENGUIN, 1986

The Penguin Krishnamurti Reader
NEW YORK: PENGUIN, 1987

On God
SAN FRANCISCO: HARPER & ROW, 1992

On Fear
SAN FRANCISCO: HARPER & ROW, 1995

The Essential Krishnamurti
SAN FRANCISCO: HARPER & ROW, 1996

The Ending of Time
WITH DR. DAVID BOHM
SAN FRANCISCO: HARPER & ROW, 1985

LAING, RONALD DAVID

Divided Self
NEW YORK: VIKING PRESS, 1991

R.D. Laing and the Paths of Anti-Psychiatry
ED., BY Z. KOTOWICZ
LONDON: ROUTLEDGE, 1997

The Politics of Experience
NEW YORK: PANTHEON, 1983

LIEDLOFF, JEAN

Continuum Concept
IN SEARCH OF HAPPINESS LOST
NEW YORK: PERSEUS BOOKS, 1986
FIRST PUBLISHED IN 1977

LOWEN, ALEXANDER

Bioenergetics
NEW YORK: COWARD, MCGOEGHAM 1975

Depression and the Body
THE BIOLOGICAL BASIS OF FAITH AND REALITY
NEW YORK: PENGUIN, 1992

Fear of Life
NEW YORK: BIOENERGETIC PRESS, 2003

Honoring the Body
THE AUTOBIOGRAPHY OF ALEXANDER LOWEN
NEW YORK: BIOENERGETIC PRESS, 2004

BIBLIOGRAPHY

Joy
THE SURRENDER TO THE BODY AND TO LIFE
NEW YORK: PENGUIN, 1995

Love and Orgasm
NEW YORK: MACMILLAN, 1965

Love, Sex and Your Heart
NEW YORK: BIOENERGETICS PRESS, 2004

Narcissism: Denial of the True Self
NEW YORK: MACMILLAN, COLLIER BOOKS, 1983

Pleasure: A Creative Approach to Life
NEW YORK: BIOENERGETICS PRESS, 2004
FIRST PUBLISHED IN 1970

The Language of the Body
PHYSICAL DYNAMICS OF CHARACTER STRUCTURE
NEW YORK: BIOENERGETICS PRESS, 2006

MILLER, ALICE

Four Your Own Good
HIDDEN CRUELTY IN CHILD-REARING AND THE ROOTS OF VIOLENCE
NEW YORK: FARRAR, STRAUS & GIROUX, 1983

Pictures of a Childhood
NEW YORK: FARRAR, STRAUS & GIROUX, 1986

The Drama of the Gifted Child
IN SEARCH FOR THE TRUE SELF
TRANSLATED BY RUTH WARD
NEW YORK: BASIC BOOKS, 1996

Thou Shalt Not Be Aware
SOCIETY'S BETRAYAL OF THE CHILD
NEW YORK: NOONDAY, 1998

The Political Consequences of Child Abuse
IN: THE JOURNAL OF PSYCHOHISTORY 26, 2 (FALL 1998)

MOORE, THOMAS

Care of the Soul
A GUIDE FOR CULTIVATING DEPTH AND SACREDNESS IN EVERYDAY LIFE
NEW YORK: HARPER & COLLINS, 1994

REICH, WILHELM

Children of the Future
ON THE PREVENTION OF SEXUAL PATHOLOGY
NEW YORK: FARRAR, STRAUS & GIROUX, 1983
FIRST PUBLISHED IN 1950

CORE (Cosmic Orgone Engineering)
PART I, SPACE SHIPS, DOR AND DROUGHT
©1984, ORGONE INSTITUTE PRESS
XEROX COPY FROM THE WILHELM REICH MUSEUM

Early Writings 1
NEW YORK: FARRAR, STRAUS & GIROUX, 1975

Ether, God & Devil & Cosmic Superimposition
NEW YORK: FARRAR, STRAUS & GIROUX, 1972
ORIGINALLY PUBLISHED IN 1949

Genitality in the Theory and Therapy of Neurosis
©1980 BY MARY BOYD HIGGINS AS DIRECTOR OF THE WILHELM REICH INFANT TRUST

People in Trouble
©1974 BY MARY BOYD HIGGINS AS DIRECTOR OF THE WILHELM REICH INFANT TRUST

BIBLIOGRAPHY

Record of a Friendship
THE CORRESPONDENCE OF WILHELM REICH AND A. S. NEILL
NEW YORK, FARRAR, STRAUS & GIROUX, 1981

Selected Writings
AN INTRODUCTION TO ORGONOMY
NEW YORK: FARRAR, STRAUS & GIROUX, 1973

The Bioelectrical Investigation of Sexuality and Anxiety
NEW YORK: FARRAR, STRAUS & GIROUX, 1983
ORIGINALLY PUBLISHED IN 1935

The Bion Experiments
REPRINTED IN *SELECTED WRITINGS*
NEW YORK: FARRAR, STRAUS & GIROUX, 1973

The Function of the Orgasm (The Orgone, Vol. 1)
ORGONE INSTITUTE PRESS, NEW YORK, 1942

The Cancer Biopathy (The Orgone, Vol. 2)
NEW YORK: FARRAR, STRAUS & GIROUX, 1973

The Invasion of Compulsory Sex Morality
NEW YORK: FARRAR, STRAUS & GIROUX, 1971
ORIGINALLY PUBLISHED IN 1932

The Leukemia Problem: Approach
©1951, ORGONE INSTITUTE PRESS
COPYRIGHT RENEWED 1979
XEROX COPY FROM THE WILHELM REICH MUSEUM

The Mass Psychology of Fascism
NEW YORK: FARRAR, STRAUS & GIROUX, 1970
ORIGINALLY PUBLISHED IN 1933

The Orgone Energy Accumulator
ITS SCIENTIFIC AND MEDICAL USE
©1951, 1979, ORGONE INSTITUTE PRESS
XEROX COPY FROM THE WILHELM REICH MUSEUM

The Schizophrenic Split
©1945, 1949, 1972 BY MARY BOYD HIGGINS AS DIRECTOR OF THE
WILHELM REICH INFANT TRUST
XEROX COPY FROM THE WILHELM REICH MUSEUM

The Sexual Revolution
©1945, 1962 BY MARY BOYD HIGGINS AS DIRECTOR OF THE WILHELM REICH
INFANT TRUST

REID, DANIEL P.

The Tao of Health, Sex & Longevity
A MODERN PRACTICAL GUIDE TO THE ANCIENT WAY
NEW YORK: SIMON & SCHUSTER, 1989

Guarding the Three Treasures
THE CHINESE WAY OF HEALTH
NEW YORK: SIMON & SCHUSTER, 1993

ROSEN, SYDNEY (ED.)

My Voice Will Go With You
THE TEACHING TALES OF MILTON H. ERICKSON
NEW YORK: NORTON & CO., 1991

STEIN, ROBERT M.

Redeeming the Inner Child in Marriage and Therapy
IN: RECLAIMING THE INNER CHILD
ED. BY JEREMIAH ABRAMS
NEW YORK: TARCHER/PUTNAM, 1990, 261 FF.

STEINER, RUDOLF

Theosophy
AN INTRODUCTION TO THE SPIRITUAL PROCESSES IN HUMAN LIFE
AND IN THE COSMOS
NEW YORK: ANTHROPOSOPHIC PRESS, 1994

STONE, HAL & STONE, SIDRA

Embracing Our Selves
THE VOICE DIALOGUE MANUAL
SAN RAFAEL, CA: NEW WORLD LIBRARY, 1989

SZASZ, THOMAS

The Myth of Mental Illness
NEW YORK: HARPER & ROW, 1984

TART, CHARLES T.

Altered States of Consciousness
A BOOK OF READINGS
HOBOKEN, N.J.: WILEY & SONS, 1969

WHAT THE BLEEP DO WE KNOW!?

See Arntz, William

Whitfield, Charles L.

Healing the Child Within
DEERFIELD BEACH, FL: HEALTH COMMUNICATIONS, 1987

PERSONAL NOTES

www.ingramcontent.com/pod-product-compliance
Lightning Source LLC
Chambersburg PA
CBHW020523290526
45786CB00002B/734